```
979.4 RUB
Rubin, Saul.
You know you're in
 California when-- :101
1076361813 FOWL
```

you know you're in
california when...

Some Other Books in the Series

You Know You're in Arizona When . . .

You Know You're in Florida When . . .

You Know You're in Georgia When . . .

You Know You're in Illinois When . . .

You Know You're in Kansas When . . .

You Know You're in Massachusetts When . . .

You Know You're in Michigan When . . .

You Know You're in Minnesota When . . .

You Know You're in New Hampshire When . . .

You Know You're in New Jersey When . . .

You Know You're in Rhode Island When . . .

You Know You're in Texas When . . .

You Know You're in Washington When . . .

You Know You're In Series

you know you're in
california when...

101 Quintessential Places, People, Events, Customs, Lingo, and Eats of the Golden State

Saul Rubin

INSIDERS' GUIDE®

GUILFORD, CONNECTICUT
AN IMPRINT OF THE GLOBE PEQUOT PRESS

To buy books in quantity for corporate use
or incentives, call **(800) 962–0973**
or e-mail **premiums@GlobePequot.com**.

INSIDERS' GUIDE®

Copyright © 2007 by Morris Book Publishing, LLC

All rights reserved. No part of this book may be reproduced or transmitted in any form by any means, electronic or mechanical, including photocopying and recording, or by any information storage and retrieval system, except as may be expressly permitted by the 1976 Copyright Act or by the publisher. Requests for permission should be made in writing to The Globe Pequot Press, P.O. Box 480, Guilford, Connecticut 06437.

Insiders' Guide is a registered trademark of Morris Book Publishing, LLC.

Illustrations by Sue Mattero

Library of Congress Cataloging-in-Publication Data
Rubin, Saul.
  You know you're in California when— : 101 quintessential places, people, events, customs, lingo, and eats of the Golden State / Saul Rubin. — 1st ed.
     p. cm. — (You know you're in series)
  ISBN-13: 978-0-7627-3745-1
  ISBN-10: 0-7627-3745-X
  1. California—Miscellanea. 2. California—Description and travel—Miscellanea. I. Title.
F861.6.R83 2007
979.4—dc22

2006039666

Manufactured in the United States of America
First Edition/First Printing

To Bethany and Naomi . . .
you know you're in my heart.

about the author

Saul Rubin knows a lot about California. He's lived there for more than half his life and worked in the state as a journalist, travel writer, and college instructor. He lives with his wife and daughter in Los Angeles, where he goes against local custom by parking his own car whenever possible.

to the reader

You know California: palm trees, redwood forests, gorgeous weather, beautiful coast, Hollywood. Yeah, that's California.

Mini malls, veggie burgers, freeways, Valley girls, and Beach Boys—OK, that's California, too.

But do you really know California? Consider the famous Hollywood sign. It represents the movie business, right? Well, it does now, but it was originally built to promote a new housing development.

And Southern California beaches. You probably think they're *always* sunny. Not so. If you hit the beach in early summer, the sun will be hidden by a thick marine layer known as June Gloom. As for the rest of the year, yeah, just wonderful.

Even Californians don't really know California. Most people traveling throughout California actually live here. They are forever exploring, discovering something new to celebrate about their home state. To live in California is to embark on a great adventure.

California is an Eden of golden sunshine. That's what draws 'em in. And so what if sometimes it's a hellish domain of earthquakes, wildfires, mudslides, and the dreaded producer of the ultimate bad hair day, the Santa Ana winds? Another great day is just around the corner.

California is such a nice place to live that people like to poke fun at Californians, probably out of jealousy. "Oh, Californians," some sniff, "they're all shallow airheads obsessed with exercising, tanning, and surfing. . . ." Ah, all right, you may be right about some of us.

But the state has some pretty smart folks, too, starting with the rocket scientists at Pasadena's Jet Propulsion Laboratory, the digital wizards of Silicon Valley, and all those Nobel laureates at the University of California.

And sometimes the big brains show off their playful side, too. The state's top two colleges have engaged in a decades-long exchange of juvenile pranks that belie the level of intelligence at both schools. The Stanford-Berkeley rivalry—yeah, that's part of California, too.

California is where people come to reinvent themselves, and just to invent stuff, period. The yo-yo, Cobb salad, and the Zamboni ice-resurfacing machine are all ours. Californians are perpetually changing things, always looking ahead to the next big thing.

So how can you really know California? This book is a good place to start. For one thing, it's trim, just like a real Californian.

More importantly, this book offers the story of 101 essential things about the Golden State. Read it and you'll start to think you actually know California. But not so fast. Just as you cry out "Eureka! I really know California now!" you'll be confounded again. The state is like its many movie star residents—seemingly familiar, forever elusive.

you know you're in
california when...

...you're caught between a rock and lots of water

On the surface it seemed like a great deal: residence on an exclusive island with stunning views of San Francisco Bay and three free meals a day.

There was a whopping downside. Your neighbors were not very nice. In fact, they were considered the worst of the worst, the nation's most dangerous criminals.

This seemingly ideal residence, you see, was Alcatraz Island, the country's most notorious jail. One you moved in here, your prospects for escape were pretty much zero. Welcome home!

They called it The Rock, a craggy outpost surrounded by turbulent waters that served as a federal prison from 1934 to 1963. Its notorious residents Included gangsters Al Capone and George "Machine Gun" Kelly as well as Robert Stroud, whose avian fetish earned him the moniker "the Birdman of Alcatraz."

With freedom a tantalizing mile-and-a-quarter swim away, and life on the island monotonously gruesome, it's not surprising that some inmates attempted unauthorized shore leaves.

There were thirty-six escape attempts during the island prison's history. Twenty-three people were caught, six were fatally shot, and two were found drowned. Five escapees were officially listed as "missing and pre-sumed drowned," since it was believed no one could survive the frigid waters and strong current and make it safely to land.

The prison was expensive to operate. Among the big-budget items was the need to ship a million gallons of fresh water to the island each week. Ultimately the prison was closed and then abandoned, and the island eventually became part of the federal park system.

Now free people everywhere flock to this prison to tour its infamous grounds. You can make reservations by calling (415) 705–5555. An interesting sidelight is that Alcatraz has the West Coast's oldest operating lighthouse.

Alcatraz Island:

The federal prison housed 1,545 inmates during its 29-year history. Now a million people a year drop by to visit.

you know you're in
california when...
...an axe makes smart people do silly things

The longtime rivalry between the University of California at Berkeley (Cal) and Stanford University in nearby Palo Alto has inspired a legacy of collegiate foolishness. Students at the two brainy schools plot lowbrow pranks every year designed to humiliate their rivals.

One time the water in a Berkeley fountain turned Stanford-red, while a Cal bear print was found stenciled on Stanford's Hoover Tower. Another year Stanford students stole a stuffed Kodiak bear from Cal's campus. It turned up several days later chained to a fountain at a San Francisco subway station, having suffered the shame of being dressed in a Stanford jersey.

Passions in the rivalry run so high that while the schools boast several Nobel Laureates, faculty and students become downright goofy about possessing a simple wooden axe. That's the trophy awarded to the victor of the annual football contest between the two schools.

The 10-pound axe with the 15-inch blade was originally bought for about $3.00, but the glory that goes with it is priceless. Each school protects the axe with elaborate security, often in secret locations. Even so, there have been a few thefts through the years.

The Axe:
Coveted trophy awarded to the winner of the annual Big Game between Cal and Stanford.

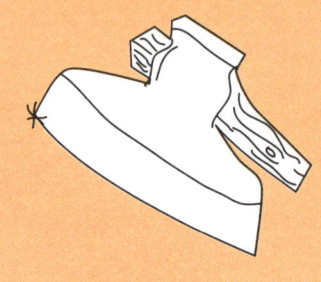

Cal students originally stole the axe from Stanford at an 1899 baseball game, then kept it locked in a bank vault for more than 30 years. Stanford students regained the axe in a 1931 caper aided by the use of tear gas.

Here's another thing that seems beneath both elite schools: You know what these deep thinkers came up with as a name for their annual big football game? The Big Game.

you know you're in
california when...
...plain vanilla just won't do

The ice cream treat that Balboa Island is famous for starts simply enough. It is a block of creamy vanilla ice cream on a stick. It's what happens next that makes the Balboa bar a legendary delight.

That vanilla ice cream is dipped in heated chocolate sauce. Then, before it cools, the bar is rolled in assorted toppings to form a sweet, crunchy coating. It is these contrasting sensations of creamy and crunchy, warm and cool, chocolate against vanilla, that make the Balboa bar one of California's prized confections.

Two shops specialize in the Balboa bar. Strangely enough, they are located just about 100 feet apart. Both claim to sell an original version of the Balboa bar. Both have oversized bananas on their storefronts to attract customers. Both have legions of fans and long lines on hot days.

Sugar 'N' Spice (310 Marine Avenue; 949–673–8907) has been in business since 1945. When the store first opened, it offered the Balboa bar dipped in only colored sprinkles or chopped peanuts. Now the store offers more exotic choices, including the popular Heath pecan crunch.

Two doors away at Dad's Donuts (318 Marine Avenue; 949–673–8686), Balboa bars can be rolled in graham cracker crumbs as well as sprinkles. Dad's opened in 1960, and it features a sign that boasts DAD'S ORIGINAL BALBOA BARS.

No one knows for sure who invented the Balboa bar. But the two shops most famous for it today are in a tasty competition to see who can perfect it.

Balboa Bars:

Balboa Island's trademark ice cream treat is a multisensory experience.

you know you're in
california when...

...even your dolls have accessorized wardrobes

Ruth Handler and her husband, Elliot, were married in Hollywood and launched the toy company Mattel in 1945. By the 1950s Ruth decided that American girls were ready for something more sophisticated in the way of dolls.

During this era girls played little mommies and cuddled with angelic baby dolls. Then Ruth showed them a teenage vamp with stiletto heels and a taste for high fashion. Playing with dolls has never been the same.

The Handlers named the doll "Barbie," after their daughter. The curvaceous, ponytailed doll made her debut at the American Toy Fair in New York in 1959 and sold for $3.00.

Ruth Handler often said that Barbie was a way for little girls to live out their dreams. The Handlers' dreams of a successful toy company were realized when Barbie went on to become the best-selling doll in history.

The Handlers later added boyfriend Ken, named after their son, and a host of other Barbie friends and assorted outfits to reflect her careers, from paleontologist to rock star.

In a strange twist, Barbie's fantasy world has frequently crossed into reality. Fashion kings such as Calvin Klein and Christian Dior have designed Barbie clothes.

Barbie Doll:

If Barbie were life-size, this California native's measurements would be an improbable 39-21-33.

Barbie has been written about in books, glorified in collector circles, and even parodied, notably on the television show *The Simpsons*. Barbie's status as an American pop culture icon was secured when she become the subject of an Andy Warhol portrait.

This is one California girl who has realized some big dreams.

you know you're in
california when...
...life is fun, fun, fun

Ah, if life were only like a Beach Boys tune from the 1960s, when it seemed that young Southern Californians enjoyed an endless summer of beach parties, great waves, cool cars, and hot romance.

Brothers Brian, Carl, and Dennis Wilson, along with cousin Mike Love and a friend, Alan Jardine, launched their distinctive sound of harmonies and innovative orchestrations in a cramped music room in a tract house in Hawthorne in 1961.

With a focus on the sunny Southern California beach lifestyle, the group rode a wave of popularity to become one of the greatest recording groups ever.

Even the British Invasion couldn't stop their frolic. The Beach Boys became the chief rival of The Beatles, with both groups inspiring one another to greater musical achievements. It was the release of the Beach Boys' monumental *Pet Sounds* recording that stirred the Beatles to create their classic *Sgt. Pepper's Lonely Heart's Club Band* album.

The California beach scene was the focal point of other musicians as well, most notably guitarist Dick Dale, who popularized the harder-edged sound of surfer music. Dale's distinctive guitar-playing captured the spirit of surfing. Meanwhile, popular singers such as Jan and Dean chimed in to celebrate surf culture too.

Beneath the romantic idealism of their music, the Beach Boys were beset by personal, artistic, and legal problems. But these couldn't diminish the value of their work. The group was enshrined in the Rock and Roll Hall of Fame in 1988.

A plaque honoring the location of the humble house in Hawthorne where the Beach Boys got their start is designated a California landmark. The house, unfortunately, is long gone, demolished to make room for a freeway.

In the plaque, the Beach Boys are pictured carrying a surfboard, set off against a more modern California soundtrack—the roar of passing cars.

The Beach Boys:

Nothing says California beach culture like the music of this distinctly California band that got its start in a Los Angeles suburb several miles from the coast.

you know you're in
california when...
...gold medals go to bronzed bodies

In the 1920s Californians took a simple ball-and-net game invented on the East Coast and shifted it from the cold gym onto the hot sand, creating beach volleyball, a sexy and very Californian form of athletics.

Yes, when a sport is played on the beach and features lots of good-looking people in skimpy bathing suits, it's a sure bet California is behind it. California has lots of recreational beach volleyball players, and the state is a major hub for the sport's professional circuit, hosting its most prestigious tournament.

Beach volleyball was first played on a Santa Monica beach and soon spread to other stretches of sand in Southern California. By the 1940s tournament play involving two-person teams was introduced on California beaches. Usually the top prize was some soda. Now the sport is booming worldwide, and its top pros compete for millions in prize money.

To followers of the sport, the Manhattan Beach Open in California is beach volleyball's Wimbledon. Begun in 1960, it is the world's longest-running beach volleyball tournament and probably the one event all the top players want to win.

That, and the Olympics. Yes, as some Olympic traditionalists cringed, beach volleyball became an Olympic sport at the 1996 Atlanta games. At the beach volleyball Olympic venue, bikini-clad dancers slither out in between points while a DJ blasts music to rock the sun-drenched crowds. Under official rules, women's uniforms are not to exceed a particular size.

Beach volleyball has clearly infused California surf culture into the ancient Olympic tradition.

Beach Volleyball:

A California sport where a winning physique counts as much as a winning score.

you know you're in
california when...

...you are fascinated by an evasive Sasquatch

A giant mystery surrounds Bigfoot, the hairy, apelike creature that some believe lurks in the wilderness areas of California's northwest.

There's evidence, all right, but most of it is of the sketchy variety, par for the course with celebrated elusive beasts. (See Loch Ness Monster and Abominable Snowman.)

The Bigfoot legend centers on scattered eyewitness accounts; a grainy, wobbly film clip; blurry photographs; alleged audio recordings; and even some physical evidence.

For the record, Bigfoot is, well, big. He's possibly 10 feet tall, weighs 500 pounds, and stands somewhat upright on extra-wide feet measuring 16 inches long. He also has long arms, smells horrid, and communicates by howling—all of which makes you wonder why a small group of true believers is so eager to find him.

News of the hulking humanoid first surfaced in 1958, when a construction worker discovered humongous footprints in a forested area north of Willow Creek. Local scribes dubbed the forest creature with really big feet "Bigfoot." Creativity with names, apparently, wasn't the newspaper's strong suit.

A brief film clip surfaced in 1967 of a furry creature ambling through an area of downed trees not far from where the original footprints were found. That fueled the Bigfoot tale. Others dismissed the film as a clumsy hoax starring a man in a monkey suit.

Count the residents of Willow Creek among the true believers. Townspeople refer to their community as the gateway to Bigfoot country. The local Willow Creek–China Flat Museum (503–629–2653) has a Bigfoot wing dedicated to the town's adopted Sasquatch, including plaster casts made from the original footprints.

Willow Creek even hosted a Bigfoot symposium that drew 200 Bigfoot fans and experts to hear evidence and consider whether the legend of Bigfoot has a leg to stand on.

Bigfoot:

The remote area north of Willow Creek is a great place for a glimpse of a hairy humanoid known for hefty feet.

you know you're in
california when...
...postcard views are everywhere

It is pretty simple to take a great photo in Big Sur. Basically, point your camera and shoot. In any direction. The only way to mess up is to leave the lens cap on.

The curvy road that threads between dramatic coastline and mountains connecting Carmel and San Simeon on Highway 1 is just one long photo opportunity, mile after mile.

Let's start with the photogenic Big Sur beaches, which are far more striking than the typical long, wide sands of Southern California. Here there are plunging cliffs, pounding surf, and idyllic hidden coves. And seemingly right on cue come frolicking otters, dolphins, elephant seals, and migrating whales to enhance any picture.

The views are equally stunning on the other side of the road. Big Sur offers thousands of acres of protected forest and wilderness, including nine state parks. Julia Pfeiffer Burns State Park (831–667–2315) has redwood trails, waterfalls, and sweeping ocean views.

Visitors to Los Padres National Forest can glimpse the rare sight of a California condor in the wild. Nearly extinct, these largest birds of North America have been introduced into the wild in Big Sur.

While nature has done a fine job with the scenery, human hands have contributed to

Big Sur:

California's most spectacular drive weaves through mountains and a wild coastline.

Big Sur's beauty as well. There's the stunning Bixby Bridge, one of the world's highest single-span concrete arch bridges. The bridge, built in 1932 and located about 15 miles south of Carmel, is 260 feet high and 700 feet long.

Sometimes the viewing here turns inward; this happens a lot at the Esalen Institute (831–667–3000; www.esalen.org). The 1960s–era retreat offers healing mineral baths and lots of personal-growth programs to nurture your spirit. Bring an open mind and a good camera.

you know you're in
california when...
...you encounter wooden whoppers

If you feel like hugging a tree in California, bring along some friends.

It would take a party of 25 folks with long arms to get their collective mitts around the General Sherman Tree, the world's biggest living thing. It soars 275 feet into the air and boasts a 103-foot girth.

The General Sherman Tree puts down roots in Sequoia National Park's Giant Forest in the state's central Sierra region. Nearby in Kings Canyon National Park, the General Grant Tree stands 268 feet tall. It is designated as the Nation's Christmas Tree. (Visit www.nps.gov/seki or call 539–565–3341 for information on both parks.)

California is truly a land of giants when it comes to trees. It is home to the world's tallest and biggest varieties, coast redwoods and giant sequoias. The coast redwoods are more slender and elegant, while the inland sequoias are more squat and bulky. Both types of tree have long life spans, exceeding 2,000 years.

While not as big in volume as the General Sherman Tree, the Mendocino Tree in Montgomery Woods (707–937–5804), about 15 miles west of Ukiah, is the world's tallest tree at 367 feet.

Many of California's big trees were harvested for lumber decades ago, but swaths of redwoods and sequoias have been preserved in several parks in the northern half of the state. Redwood National Park (707–464–6101) in the north coastal area is a prime spot for viewing tall trees. So are Muir Woods National Monument (415–388–2595), north of San Francisco, and Humboldt Redwoods State Park (707–946–2409), north of Garberville. For a unique blend of roadside kitsch and wondrous nature, take a spin on the Avenue of the Giants, a 31-mile portion of Old Highway 101 that stretches from Garberville to Ferndale. This tour features many curious tourist attractions along with some of the state's biggest trees, including several that you can drive through in Myers Flat, Leggett, and Klamath.

Big Trees:

California's big trees are natural skyscrapers.

you know you're in
california when...
...you live life in the very slow lane

The bristlecone pine tree's secret for a long life is not to hurry along the journey. This strange tree goes through life at such a sluggish pace it seems like it almost isn't living at all. It's just being there.

The bristlecone takes the notion of slow growth to an extreme. In a span of one hundred years, it may add only an inch to its girth. It dies slowly too, sometimes clinging to life through a single, gnarled strip of bark that endures for centuries.

Making their life's passage at this listless rate, the bristlecone pines of California have earned recognition as the world's oldest living things. (Some of them first sprouted almost 5,000 years ago.) These senior trees are found in the Ancient Bristlecone Pine Forest located in the Inyo National Forest in the state's eastern Sierra region.

One of the oldest trees here was given the appropriately ancient name of Methuselah. Scientist Edmund Schulman, who estimated at the time that the tree was 4,723 years old, discovered it in 1957. Now scientists believe that other trees in the area are even older, but they don't publicize their locations in order to protect them from intruders.

If you want to pay your respects to these elders, stop by the Schulman Grove Visitor Center (760–873–2500) in the Inyo National Forest north of Big Pine. Access into the area is usually limited to mid-May through October because of bad weather during winter and early spring.

Life may be long for the bristlecone pine, but it isn't sweet. The soil is undernourished, and there is little rainfall. The area's high elevation promotes torturous winds and widely variable temperatures that make for one harsh existence.

The grotesque shapes of some of these trees reflect their lifelong struggles. Many of them are bent at odd angles, giving them the appearance of abstract wooden sculptures set against a barren, lunar-like landscape. Needless to say, this otherworldly forest is a photographer's paradise.

Bristlecone Trees:

The world's oldest living things picked a pretty harsh place to live in California.

you know you're in
california when...
...you talk a good game

The phrase "It's in the refrigerator" might not be cause for celebration in most parts of the world. But in Los Angeles that pronouncement meant it was time to celebrate another victory by the Lakers basketball team.

That's what longtime Lakers announcer Chick Hearn would declare when he felt a win was locked up, even with game time remaining. The full phrase went: "The door's closed, the lights are out, the eggs are cooling, the butter's getting hard, and the Jell-O is jiggling."

The refrigerator riff is just one of dozens of "Chickisms" that peppered Hearn's staccato delivery during a Hall of Fame career. The list of Chickisms could fill a book. Many are now staples of basketball language, including "air ball" (when a shot misses everything) and "slam dunk" (when a player slams the ball directly through the hoop).

Others popular among Lakers fans were: "The mustard's off the hot dog" (when a player made a mistake trying to be too showy); and "He faked him into the popcorn machine" (when a defensive player looked foolish because of a clever offensive move).

Hearn, who died in 2002, announced a record 3,338 consecutive Lakers games, a streak that ended in 2001 when he had heart surgery.

Broadcast Legends:

Three legendary California sports announcers have scored big with fans.

Meanwhile, another Los Angeles broadcasting legend, Vin Scully, voice of the Los Angeles Dodgers, keeps on going. Scully has a decidedly more mellow approach than Hearn. If Hearn was basketball's version of a hip-hop singer, Vin Scully is baseball's concert pianist. His melodic tones and smooth delivery have calmed and informed Dodger fans for more than five decades and earned him recognition as one of the greatest sports announcers ever.

Up north, announcer Bill King entertained fans for many years as the well-known voice of three Bay Area professional sports teams, including the Oakland Raiders, popularizing the slogan, "Holy Toledo!"

When it comes to sports broadcasting, Hearn, Scully, and King are clearly in a league of their own.

you know you're in
california when...
...you don't throw your gum away

In the heart of California's central coast is a landmark so yucky that people just have to see it. It's a narrow alley in downtown San Luis Obispo with both facing walls smeared with thousands of wads of chewed gum.

Most people are grossed out when they first hear about it, and then, surprisingly, intrigued. Bubble Gum Alley is a major tourist draw to gum-smacking visitors in this college town with a sophomoric sense of humor in its civic monuments.

The alley is located in the 700 block of Higuera Street. The walls, about 15 feet high and 70 feet long, are covered with thousands of small wads of gum.

Some of the gum wads are quite filthy, if you need anything else to make the scene more distasteful in your mind. But others are more artistically arranged, with some shaped to form pictures or words, such as a flower or a friendly "Hi!"

Bubble Gum Alley is a San Luis Obispo tradition that dates to the 1950s. No one is quite sure how it got started, and some locals aren't pleased that it did. After all, it takes special vision to declare walls of wadded gum a treasured example of local culture.

Bubble Gum Alley:

What is probably the world's most gross civic landmark is found in Central California.

Every so often a vocal anti-gum movement emerges in town and there are cries to wash it all away and return to more sanitary forms of gum disposal. One year a hose was turned on the wall for just that purpose, but it only created more of a mess, so the clean-up was halted.

Bubble Gum Alley is sticking around.

you know you're in
california when...
...you stand up to any bull

The arrival of spring in the Central Valley means it's bullfighting time. Not bullfighting in the traditional Spanish sense, with the cut-off ears and the spilling of blood and all that. This is bullfighting with a California twist.

California's version of bullfighting is less intense than the traditional sport as practiced in Mexico and Spain. It still involves climbing into a ring with an agitated 1,000-pound bull, so there's nothing wimpy about it.

Here the bull lives to be agitated another day, although he might be headed to the slaughterhouse in the end anyway. But first the bull endures being hit with Velcro darts thrust onto a patch strapped to its brawny shoulders. The pointy horns of the bull are also rounded off and then covered in leather to make them less dangerous.

In a display of courage worthy of any matador, a part of California's bullfighting tradition consists of teams of young men that wrestle the bulls to the ground. They like to call the sport here "bloodless bullfighting." Bloodless for the bull, maybe, but not necessarily for these at-risk performers, who sometimes suffer broken limbs, scrapes, bruises, and the occasional concussion.

Real bullfighting was banned in California in 1947, but the state permits bullfights as part of religious celebrations. In several Central Valley farming towns from May through October, the Portuguese community presents the bullfights as part of religious festivals.

Pure passion for the sport motivates others in California to learn real bullfighting skills at the California Academy of Tauromaquia in San Diego (619–709–0664; www.bullfightschool.com), America's first bullfighting school. The first time a beginner sees action in the ring here he or she will probably face off against a person dressed like a bull. Budding matadors then graduate to live animals with a trip across the border to a training site in Mexico, where it's legal to fight real bulls.

Bullfighting:
This macho sport has a strong presence in California.

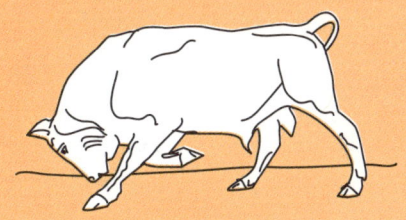

you know you're in california when...

...you have a very green thumb

To Luther Burbank, a rose was never just a rose. Then again, neither was an apple just an apple, nor a potato just a potato.

In Burbank's view anything that grew from the ground could always use a little improvement. Or be changed entirely. He once crossbred apricots with plums to create the plumcot.

In more than five decades of botanical wizardry, Burbank created more than 800 varieties of new plants, from exquisite roses to a studly potato that bears his name. The Russet-Burbank is the most commonly grown spud in America.

Burbank was born in Massachusetts but discovered his true calling in California. He migrated to Santa Rosa in 1875 while in his twenties, finding the soil and climate ideal for his gardening experiments. He later bought additional land in nearby Sebastopol so he could have more soil to use as his laboratory. Inspired by Darwin, Burbank set out to make crops taste better, grow faster, or look more beautiful in the garden.

He was sort of a Dr. Frankenstein with fertilizer, but his results were a lot prettier. And good-tasting, too. He developed dozens of new plums, including the incredibly flavorful Santa Rosa variety. Burbank was obsessed with creating the ideal daisy and spent 17 years perfecting his Shasta variety, a classy flower with snow-white petals.

His two Northern California properties are historic landmarks open year-round to visitors. The best times to visit are when most things are blooming in spring and summer; special tours are offered then.

The Burbank Home and Gardens is located at Santa Rosa and Sonoma Avenues in Santa Rosa (707–524–7781). The Luther Burbank Gold Ridge Experiment Farm is at 7781 Bodega Avenue in Sebastopol (707–823–5998).

California recognizes Burbank's achievements in the garden by designating his birthday, March 7, as the state's Arbor Day.

Burbank, Luther:

The city of Santa Rosa hosts the Luther Burbank Rose Parade and Festival (707–542–7673) on the third Saturday of every May.

you know you're in
california when...

...public transportation is more fun than an amusement park ride

San Francisco's cable cars are America's most amusing form of public transportation. Millions of people ride them not to get anywhere, but just for the fun of it. Imagine saying that about a bus.

The cable cars have survived earthquakes, political attacks, and the arrival of faster, more efficient ways of moving people from one place to another. It's hard to imagine the San Francisco landscape without its cable cars climbing "halfway to the stars," as the musical tribute goes.

Andrew Hallidie created the city's first cable cars in 1873, believing them an improvement over horse-drawn cars, which often struggled up the city's steep hills.

Buses eventually replaced some of the cable car lines and it looked like the cars would clang off into history. In 1947 San Francisco Mayor Roger Lapham proposed scrapping all the remaining lines in favor of more advanced "superbuses"—bigger and more powerful dual-engine buses.

But a strong citizen campaign saved the cars. Today three cable car lines operate up and down some of the city's steepest hills, offering great views and a bit of an amusement park thrill as a bonus. Seats on outside benches are coveted spots.

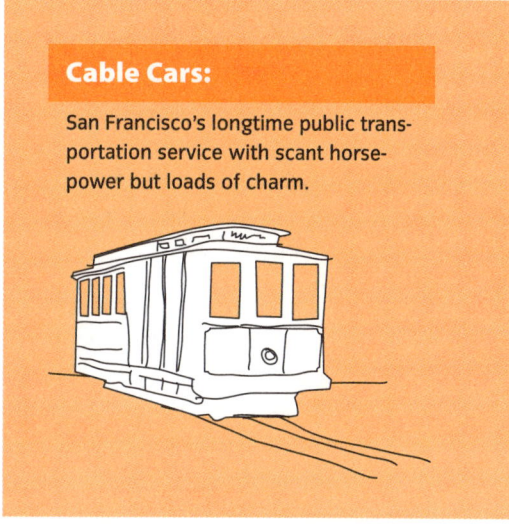

Cable Cars:

San Francisco's longtime public transportation service with scant horsepower but loads of charm.

If you want a peek beneath the outer charms of the cable car lines, head to the Cable Car Museum (1201 Mason Street; 415–474–1887). Displays trace the history of the city's cable cars, while a downstairs area houses the powerful pulleys that turn the underground cables that propel the cars.

Each July cable car operators showcase their talents in Union Square at a bell-ringing contest, an event first held in 1949. The honking of Lapham's proposed "superbuses" just wouldn't sound the same.

you know you're in
california when...

...your entree looks like an abstract painting

If your meal arrives and you find yourself wondering whether to eat it or frame it, chances are you're contemplating a just-prepared specimen of California cuisine.

California cuisine demands that food not only taste good, but look fabulous, too. (This *is* California, after all.)

The start of California cuisine can be traced to a kitchen in Berkeley. That's where chef Alice Waters opened Chez Panisse (1517 Shattuck Avenue: 510–548–5525) in 1971. Waters just said "Non!" to the creamy, fat-laden European style of cooking popular at the time and took a lighter, more Californian approach.

Waters stressed dishes made with organic, fresh ingredients combined in exotic, creative ways. This being California, fresh vegetables and seasonings were readily available.

Citrus flavorings became a trademark. Vegetables once stuck in the back of produce bins gathering mold were suddenly thrust into starring roles. Artichokes, for example, were being tossed into several dishes, including pizza.

Yes, pizza. Wolfgang Puck added his spin on California cuisine with the opening in the early 1980s of Spago in West Hollywood, since moved to Beverly Hills (176 North Canon Drive: 310–385–0880). He became famous for his wild ideas about what to put on pizza and has played a big role in bringing California cuisine to the masses.

While Puck added more European and Asian touches to his cooking, California cuisine in the end is very much Californian—stylish, trendy, and healthy, and looking pretty as a picture on your plate.

> **California Cuisine:**
> A style of cooking launched in California in the 1970s that is a feast for the eyes as well as the stomach.

you know you're in
california when...
...that barking you hear isn't from a dog

California sea lions are blubbery contradictions. They're wild animals but very intelligent. They're cute and cuddly but at times ferocious and destructive.

They don't make the best neighbors, considering that they spew fishy excrement and bark loudly and often. Fishermen despise them, since the wily hunters often steal their catch.

But in California there is no escaping the sea lions, since, well, the sea lions kind of take the initiative here. They've been coming ashore for decades, sometimes wreaking havoc at boat docks and harbors, and at times delighting humans with their playful antics.

The most famous sea lion invasion began in 1989 at the tourist destination Pier 39 (www.pier39.com) in San Francisco. Sea lions began "hauling out" on a boat dock there, spreading foul odors and making life unpleasant for boaters.

Pier shop owners at first cursed the rowdy mammals, but then wised up when they realized the sea lions were attracting quite a crowd. The boat owners were sent elsewhere and the sea lions were welcomed as honored guests.

Sometimes hundreds of sea lions can be viewed at the dock as they huddle in mounds or waddle about and posture. They occasionally engage in playful fighting, or even real, albeit clumsy, combat. Pier operators have built viewing stands for people, and everyone is happy about the arrangement.

Elsewhere in California sea lion encounters have not turned out so well. Sea lions have attempted takeovers of boats and docks in places such as Newport and Monterey, but the mammals haven't received as warm a welcome there. Officials have instead tried to fend them off with a variety of methods, including squirt guns, rubber bullets, and fake killer whales. Stronger methods to repel them are unlawful—sea lions were granted federal protection in 1972. The way they move about freely on land, these smart and determined creatures act like they know they are above the law.

California Sea Lions:

These crafty, charming wild mammals prefer docks to rocks for prolonged rests.

you know you're in
california when...
...you bathe in mud

Calistoga is a Napa Valley resort town famous for its therapeutic tubs of steamy muck. Here the term "mud bath" is not an oxymoron but a major tourist draw.

Local spas invite guests to ease into the ooze, a restorative and lumpy mixture of local volcanic ash and bubbly mineral water touted for its powers to soothe nerves and rejuvenate weary souls.

Sam Brannan opened the town's first mud bath spa in the 1860s. Brannan's goal was to make the town the "Saratoga of California." As the story goes, Brannan might have celebrated a little too much at the dedication ceremony and apparently slurred his words to reporters, who heard him say he was building the "Calistoga of Sarafornia." The drunken mispronunciation stuck.

A wary public took some time to warm to the idea of soaking in balmy goop as a way to feel good. Europeans more familiar with the concept helped popularize Calistoga's mud baths in the 1920s. A few decades later the area became a haven for arthritis sufferers.

Today Calistoga's mud enjoys a rock-solid reputation as a legitimate spa treatment. For a list of Calistoga's spas, contact the city's Chamber of Commerce at 707–942–6333 or visit its Web site at www.calistogafun.com.

Thousands flock here each year for the privilege of squirming into basins filled with hot mud until they are covered to their necks in mire. Exclamations of "Eeew!" quickly turn to "Ahhhh." A short mud bath is usually followed by more conventional methods of tension release: mineral water baths and massages.

Locals insist that the area's unique geothermal properties make its mud much more than ordinary soggy dirt. They claim it cleanses the body of toxins, relieves tension, and even exfoliates. Now, that's special mud.

Calistoga Mud Baths:

Health-inducing immersions in mud produced from local mineral water and volcanic soil.

you know you're in
california when...
...you can stargaze in broad daylight

To cap off her celebration for winning the Best Actress award for 2004, Hilary Swank opted for a late-night stop at a West Hollywood burger stand, a humble venue far removed from the glitz of other Oscar-themed bashes.

If you happened to be there that evening chowing down on a patty melt and fries, you would have been treated to a most unexpected sighting of the glamorous Swank clutching her Oscar statuette and ordering up some fast-food grub.

Celebrity sightings are a common pastime in the Los Angeles area, where the Hollywood elite are densely packed.

Sightings can occur in the most mundane locales. I once rode with Ray Charles in a medical office elevator on my way to see a doctor about a sinus infection. It almost made the pulsing pain worth it. I encountered Jamie Lee Curtis twice—at a chiropractor's office and also in a supermarket produce section.

Some celebrity hunters increase their odds of success by flocking to trendy star hangouts. Of course, these sites change almost weekly, and you'll have to fight the crowds and the paparazzi to get a good look.

Out-of-towners are often coaxed into buying "star maps," street guides that show where local stars reside. Buyers of these

Celebrity Sightings:

Stay in the Los Angeles area long enough and chances are you'll spot a famous face.

maps cruise areas such as Beverly Hills hoping for a live-in-the-flesh glimpse of a favorite icon. They are mostly rewarded with views of tall hedges, security gates, and empty driveways.

A sure sign of a tourist or newcomer is a person wildly pointing or shrieking at a just-spotted celebrity as if the star were some kind of exotic animal encountered in the wild. The unwritten local rule is to act cool and offer a more subdued nod or casual smile, or even a benign comment such as, "Love your work!"

Then allow the besieged celebrity to get back to whatever mundane task he or she was doing, such as picking out a ripe melon at the store.

you know you're in
california when...
...the year of the rat is something to celebrate

Every dog has his day in San Francisco. So do the rats, monkeys, and roosters.

It's all part of the fun of celebrating the Chinese New Year in San Francisco's Chinatown, America's largest and most historic Chinese-American community. The Chinese calendar is based on twelve zodiac animals, which also include pigs and dragons.

Whatever animal is featured, the Chinese New Year ignites a two-week celebration in San Francisco that includes firecrackers, street festivals, and a parade that's been a tradition here since 1860. The parade highlight is the appearance of a 200-foot dragon controlled by a hundred martial arts experts, no easy task.

In Southern California there is a noted Chinatown north of downtown Los Angeles and other major Chinese-American centers in San Gabriel and Monterey Park.

But San Francisco's Chinatown is the state's major tourist draw, receiving more annual visitors than the Golden Gate Bridge. With no offense to tourists, though, this is a community that exists foremost for itself. The Chinese-themed herb shops, temples, banks, and markets are not here just for show or tourist photo ops. They are used daily by the thousands of people who live, work, and shop here.

From the imposing Chinese gate at Grant Avenue and Bush Street, to the many street lanterns and Chinese signs and shops, Chinatown is a feast for the eyes. It is also a place for feasting, period.

Chinatown offers many restaurants where the last course is a small, twisted cookie that offers a fortune. Fortune cookies were invented in San Francisco around 1920, based on an ancient Chinese military practice of passing secret messages hidden in special cakes.

Stop by the Golden Gate Fortune Cookie Company (56 Ross Alley; 415–781–3956) and watch as workers continue the tradition of making the cookies by hand. Here you can take fate into your own hands by ordering cookies stuffed with your own message.

Chinatown:

San Francisco's Chinatown feels like home for many Chinese-Americans.

you know you're in
california when...

...you're caught in a chocolate swirl

While Californians enjoy a reputation for healthy eating habits, chocolate apparently is an accepted indulgence. The state is a chocolate lover's paradise.

Five chocolate manufacturers are located in Northern California alone, nearly half the number in the entire country. Meanwhile, dozens of candy makers large and small dot the state like so many chocolate sprinkles.

California got an early lesson in cocoa cuisine from Domingo Ghirardelli, who opened a chocolate plant and shop in San Francisco in 1852. He was quite successful. Forty-niners had not only a nose for gold but a sweet tooth as well. And the Bay Area's cool weather proved a valuable asset because chocolate has an annoying tendency to melt when warm.

Today, Ghirardelli (800–877–9338; www.ghirardelli.com) is the longest continuously operating chocolate maker in America, beating out another venerable Bay Area producer, Guittard (800–468–2462; www.guittard.com). Both companies now are based just outside San Francisco. You can still see equipment from Ghirardelli's original chocolate manufactory at Ghirardelli Square in San Francisco at 900 North Point Street.

See's (800–347–7337; www.sees.com) is one of the state's treasured resources, a candy maker that first opened in Los Angeles in 1921. With its pristine black-and-white decor and candy sellers outfitted in pure white, See's shop turns this sinful indulgence into a heavenly experience.

A new entry in the chocolate business is Scharffen Berger (510–981–4050; www.scharffenberger.com), founded in Berkeley in 1994 by partners Robert Steinberg and champagne maker John Scharffenberger. They first worked out chocolate recipes in a kitchen using, among other devices, a coffee grinder and hair dryer. Don't ask. Just trust that these men are serious about their chocolate.

Oakdale, home of the Hershey's Visitor Center (209–848–8126) hosts an annual chocolate festival on the third weekend in May. A stroll down the festival's Chocolate Avenue is akin to entering a Willy Wonka fantasyland.

> **Chocolate:**
> A favorite treat in California, where chocolate makers and candy makers keep life sweet.

you know you're in
california when...
...salad is so much more than just lettuce

Robert Cobb entered the kitchen of his Brown Derby restaurant in Los Angeles in 1937 looking to satisfy a late-night hunger.

For the record—and it's important to the story—what Cobb scrounged up that night was: chicken, bacon, cheese, avocado, hard-boiled egg, tomatoes, lettuce, and chives. He chopped them up and tossed them in a bowl with French dressing.

The impromptu salad was filling and tasty. News of such a fine salad spread quickly in Los Angeles, as word of any new good thing does. Pretty soon Derby diners began requesting the Cobb salad and an American culinary classic was born.

There are as many versions today of the Cobb salad as there are versions of how the salad was actually created. Some stories have Cobb making the first salad not for himself but for Hollywood theater owner Sid Grauman. It was Grauman who became the salad's biggest fan and promoter.

Another story is that Cobb made his first Cobb salad because he had a toothache and he didn't want to chew on anything too big. However it started, the Cobb became the signature dish at the Derby, a legendary Los Angeles hangout that opened in 1926.

Cobb Salad:

The Cobb salad was created in California in one mad dash to quench a late-night hunger, so the story goes.

Eventually there were four Brown Derby restaurants in Los Angeles, including one shaped like a hat. The latter featured a neon sign that read: EAT IN THE HAT. The Derby was where Hollywood's elite gathered to drink and dine. Clark Gable even proposed to Carole Lombard there.

The restaurants are all closed now, the chain's salad days long gone. But the Brown Derby's famous salad lives on.

you know you're in
california when...
...people on horses shout "Yahoo!"

In its day Pioneertown saw more Wild West action than any other place in California, including posse chases, shootouts, and saloon brawls. When the action was over, someone always yelled "Cut!" Then the cowboys dusted themselves off and probably broke for lunch.

Pioneertown's heyday doesn't even go as far back as the real Old West. The town was built in 1946 to play the part of an Old West town. Dozens of westerns were made here and then Hollywood packed up and left. That's when real people moved in.

Today Pioneertown (www.pioneertown.com) is a small tourist community that stages shootouts on its Main Street from April through November and exists as probably the only town in the world that wasn't built to be a real place.

Another popular California location for westerns was the Alabama Hills near Lone Pine. The region is now home to the Lone Pine Film Festival (760–876–9103), one of the world's most unique film events. The festival, held each fall, screens only films shot on location in Lone Pine. You can watch a movie and then tour the nearby location where the film was shot.

Despite the influence of Hollywood, not all cowboys in California are from central casting. Some are genuine. On the ranchos of pre-California, Spanish buckaroos called *vaqueros* did plenty of real riding and roping. Each spring modern riders pay tribute to the vaqueros' skills at the Californios Ranch Roping and Stock Horse Contest (530–896–9566) in Red Bluff, which also hosts a traditional rodeo.

Oakdale, which calls itself the "Cowboy Capital of the World," holds an annual rodeo and also has a cowboy museum (209–847–5163) that offers the "sights, sounds, and smells" of the Wild West. The smells, presumably, come from many of the saddles on display here.

The biggest real cowboy rodeo event in the state is the California Rodeo in Salinas (831–775–3100). Unlike the action in westerns, when a cowboy goes down here, it really smarts.

Cowboy Culture:
California has lots of real and pretend cowboys.

you know you're in
california when...
...sporting events sport a whole new look

They play baseball in California. And football, basketball, and a bunch of other traditional sports.

And then things get a little weird. California hosts dozens of competitive events that are downright ridiculous.

Let's start with the Humboldt Kinetic Sculpture race, a pseudo bike race that is actually a golden opportunity for locals to express their artistic sides. The race, held every Memorial Day weekend since 1969, features a wild assortment of sculptures on wheels that are pedaled along a 38-mile land-and-water course. There are lots of photos at the event's Web site at www.kineticsculpturerace.org.

Looks count just as much in San Francisco's Bay to Breakers race (415–359–2800; www.baytobreakers.com), which began in 1912 as a traditional road race but has since veered way off course. This race, essentially an annual Mardi Gras in sneakers, doesn't go to the swiftest but the ones with the most outrageous costumes.

San Francisco also hosts the annual Urban Iditarod (www.urbaniditarod.com), a race held at the same time as the real Alaskan mush race. Beyond that, there are no similarities to the actual event.

Mushers maneuver shopping carts through the snowless urban course, hauled by hapless human sled teams. There are frequent stops for refreshments at taverns conveniently located along the race route.

The Sugar Bowl resort in Lake Tahoe (www.sugarbowl.com) hosts the annual Tiki Cup, an unlikely combination of Polynesian culture and alpine racing. Spectators are served mai tais from iced canoes to help them overcome the culture clash of seeing skiers in grass skirts.

Other events off the charts include the annual Pillow Fighting Championships in Kenwood (www.kenwoodpillowfights.com), where a pajama party standby is elevated to the status of a (somewhat) competitive sport every July 4th, and the Gar Woods annual Polar Bear Swim (www.garwoods.com), a 200-yard winter dash in frigid Lake Tahoe.

Crazy Sports:

The wide world of sports in California is very wide indeed.

you know you're in
california when...
...you don't often come out of your shell

The desert tortoise, California's state reptile, may be slow afoot but it is ultra-swift when it comes to survival skills.

It takes a cagey reptile to tough it out in California's Mojave Desert, a most unforgiving place. The desert tortoise's primary home is parched land that features scorching summers and bone-chilling winters.

The key to desert survival can be summed up in one word: water. Here's where the desert tortoise is particularly crafty. Tortoises use their sharp claws and strong, elephantlike legs to dig basins in the soil to catch water. They return to these basins at the first hint of rain to get a well-deserved drink. That's good planning.

The tortoise has learned to make do with very little, another key to domestic bliss in the desert. Home for the desert tortoise is a simple burrow dug out of sandy soil with space enough to accommodate their typical foot-long bodies.

Desert tortoises conserve energy by hibernating from early fall until spring. They emerge at other times mostly to eat, drink, and mate. Occasionally males battle each other for dominance, the loser being the tortoise who gets turned upside down. Then the excitement is over and everyone goes back to basic survival mode.

Even with these keen survival skills, the desert tortoise is having a rough time. It is

Desert Tortoise:

California's state reptile can live for up to 100 years, if it survives predators and a harsh environment.

listed as threatened under the Endangered Species Act. Tortoises are particularly vulnerable during their first five years of life, when they are often turned into meals by various desert predators. People haven't been so nice either, encroaching upon the tortoises' habitat and sometimes running over their burrows or the tortoises themselves with their vehicles.

Conservationists have built a 40-square-mile protection zone in the Mojave National Preserve called the Desert Tortoise Natural Area (760–252–6100). This is the best place to see the tortoises in their natural environment. Prime viewing times are spring and summer.

you know you're in
california when...
...a New York rivalry still simmers out west

Californians are a famously laid-back sort—polar opposites, say, from New Yorkers. But Californians have done their best to fan the flames of a heated and longtime baseball rivalry that they inherited from the Big Apple.

When the Dodgers and Giants played each other as cross-borough rivals in New York, it was less like baseball and more like going to war with gloves, bats, and balls. Each game determined New York bragging rights.

Then after the 1957 season, the Dodgers left Ebbets Field in Brooklyn to play in Los Angeles, while the Giants bid farewell to the Polo Grounds and headed to San Francisco. California meetings between the Giants and Dodgers often feel more like genuine baseball games and less like the life-and-death battles they were back in New York, but those appearances can be deceiving.

Fans and players on both sides muster up appropriate passion for these diamond clashes, making Giants–Dodgers games special events on the California sports calendar.

When the Dodgers travel to San Francisco, fans will rally the stadium with heartfelt chants of "Beat L.A.!" Dodger fans in Los Angeles, often more focused on leaving games early to beat the traffic, stick around in greater numbers when the Giants are in town.

In fact, the ugliest incident in Giants-Dodgers history happened in California in 1965. That's when Giants pitcher Juan Marichal bloodied up Dodgers catcher John Roseboro by hitting him over the head with a bat. Yes, that New York intensity is still evident in California.

Dodgers–Giants Rivalry:

Since migrating to California, the Giants–Dodgers rivalry has maintained its New York edge.

you know you're in
california when...
...all your faults are buried underground

California has a glaring, geologic imperfection. It seems that the southern half is pushing toward the northern half. One day, Los Angeles and San Francisco will be neighbors.

That impending culture clash is about fifteen million years away. The more immediate fallout from all this underground jostling is that California is a hot zone for earthquakes. California experiences more than half a million seismic tremors each year, although only about 150 can be felt and it is rare that they cause damage.

Still, it is unsettling to know that the Big One could hit at any moment, at a most inconvenient moment, maybe a soap-in-the-eyes shower kind of moment. Somehow, though, Californians eschew a constant duck-and-cover panic mode and go about their daily lives as if blissfully ignorant of the perilous shadow they live under.

Some find comfort in telltale signs. Aunt Martha's cat acting weird? Still air and unusually hot weather? Get ready because an earthquake is coming for sure.

Geologists pooh-pooh such intuitive notions as bad science, although they confidently predict that the next Big One will strike California sometime before 2030. Or maybe not.

All of which makes for some sleepless nights. Or you can just have fun with it, as do the folks in the tiny central Californian town of Parkfield. Parkfield lies right on the San Andreas Fault and has experienced a major earthquake every twenty years or so since the 1850s. Quakes happen here with such frequency that scientists consider the town a regular earthquake laboratory.

Is anyone here worried? Nope. A merry sign on the town's water tower cheerfully proclaims Parkfield the EARTHQUAKE CAPITAL OF THE WORLD. The town's cafe offers items such as the Big One, a one-pound sirloin, and desserts known as "aftershocks."

The town's motto, which could go for all Californians, is "Be Here When It Happens."

Earthquakes:
A constant threat in California that might rattle your nerves if you gave it too much thought.

you know you're in
california when...
...the winner takes all

Watching male elephant seals engage in blubbery combat is a popular winter pastime in California. Much is at stake here, as the victor gets to mate with lovely female elephant seals. All of them. The losers? Well, they can only hope to pick up a stray conquest or wait until next year.

The fighting is quite a body-slamming spectacle. The two-ton males rear up, belch ferociously, and then ram each other in a determined quest to be the alpha male.

While brute force often wins the day, sometimes all that's needed to determine who is king of the beach is a showy pose of a male's large, pendulous nose, from which the elephant seals get their name.

Hunted almost to extinction in the 1800s, elephant seals began returning to California in the 1950s. Today a major breeding ground is the Año Nuevo State Reserve north of Santa Cruz (650–879–2025), which attracts thousands of visitors. Another popular spot is Piedras Blancas, about 7 miles north of San Simeon (805–924–1028).

Epic seal battles are only part of the show. Winter is also birthing time, and people marvel as new pups act cute and fatten themselves up for their eventual plunge into the sea.

Elephant seals are true to their name in that they are big. Males can measure up to 16 feet long. Females are smaller, although *smaller* is a relative term with elephant seals as even the females can weigh up to a ton and reach 12 feet in length. Females are just as noisy as males, often squabbling with other females over breeding spots.

Elephant seals can be spotted in California during the spring and summer, when they come ashore to endure periods of massive hair and skin loss known as molting. They mostly lie around on the beach, occasionally shifting their massive bodies to find more comfortable spots to rest. Inert, they are still quite a sight.

Elephant Seals:

These giant mounds of blubber stage quite a show every winter in California, which is mating season.

you know you're in
california when...
...your highs and lows are extreme in nature

In California it's possible to go from sitting on top of the world to the lowest of the low in a couple of hours.

We're not talking about someone's Hollywood career but a drastic change in nature that unfolds in central California's eastern region. That's where you'll find Death Valley National Park and Mount Whitney. Talk about your environmental odd couple. These two locales are about as far apart in climate as Mars and Venus, but they are separated by only 90 miles.

Death Valley is an overheated desert that contains the lowest point in North America, Badwater, at 282 feet below sea level. You'd have to dive into the sea to get any lower.

Then there is Mount Whitney, which soars almost 15,000 feet into the air, making it the highest point in the contiguous United States.

In Death Valley your umbrella will gather dust: Annual rainfall is less than 2 inches. The Valley is also one of the hottest places on earth, with summer temperatures hovering around 120 degrees Fahrenheit. On July 10, 1913, the needle went even higher—to 134 degrees—at the appropriately named Furnace Creek, setting an American record.

Leave the Valley for Mount Whitney and in a short time you'll go from sizzling desert to

Elevation Swings:

Need a big change in scenery? Make the short trip from Death Valley National Park to Mount Whitney and you'll get your wish.

an alpine setting. The mountain is prone to all kinds of snowy and icy perils during winter.

Extreme-long-distance runners take advantage of the proximity of Death Valley and Mount Whitney to run one of the world's most grueling races, the Badwater Ultramarathon. While most people just shake their heads when they hear about it, a few dozen runners actually turn up for this improbable 135-mile run from the valley's low point to more than 8,000 feet up Mount Whitney in the heat of summer.

you know you're in
california when...
...the world comes to you

You could hassle with passports and plane flights and money exchanges and language barriers to experience life in different countries. Or you could just come to California.

California is home to many ethnic enclaves that offer visitors small versions of foreign lands.

Within a few miles of downtown Los Angeles you can wander into Koreatown, Filipinotown, Little Persia, Little Ethiopia, Little Armenia, and Little Tokyo. These communities offer the flavor of their home countries in the form of their residents, restaurants, shops, and cultural events.

Little Tokyo in Los Angeles, for example, is home to the Japanese American National Museum, the only American museum dedicated to the experience of Japanese-Americans (369 East First Street; 213–625–0414). Another resource is the West Coast Players David Henry Hwang Theater, the country's first Asian-American theater group (213–625–7000).

The worldly tour continues in Little Phnom Penh in Long Beach, which has the largest population of Cambodians living outside that Asian nation. In the Orange County cities of Westminster and Garden Grove you'll find Little Saigon, home to a large number of Vietnamese.

These ethnic enclaves offer familiar comforts to new immigrants, but often with an American twist. The entrance to Thai Town in Los Angeles, for example, a mile-long section of Hollywood Boulevard, is marked by a Thai food take-out eatery that has a giant hot dog perched on its roof.

And one of Thai Town's most popular restaurants, Palms Thai (5900 Hollywood Boulevard; 323–462–5073), features entertainment by an impersonator known as the Thai Elvis.

But other elements of Thai Town are purely Thai, including its annual Songkran New Year's Festival held each April, when several blocks of Hollywood Boulevard are shut down and turned into a mini Thailand. There are booths offering Thai food and crafts as well as music and dance performances and even kickboxing demonstrations. And you can marvel as fruit and vegetable carvers turn everything from watermelons to carrots into various animal and flower shapes.

Ethnic Enclaves:

California has lots of "Little" communities.

you know you're in
california when...
...you get your kicks from simple toys

California is a trendsetter when it comes to taking remarkably simple pleasures and turning them into sensations.

California is the birthplace of the hula hoop, the Frisbee, and the yo-yo. All three were descendants of playthings that had been around for a long time. They became incredibly popular after they were developed and promoted in California.

The Frisbee was introduced in 1957 as the Pluto Platter by California's Wham-O company. Throwing discs around for fun was not new—people had been horsing around for decades by tossing around assorted metal lids, from pie tins to can tops. But the Frisbee became a big hit.

A year later Wham-O scored again with the hula hoop, an idea that dates as far back as ancient Egypt.

The modern yo-yo was introduced by Pedro Flores in Los Angeles in the 1920s, but even he claimed it was based on a toy that had been used for centuries in his native Phillipines.

These toys were cleverly marketed, however, and kids went crazy for them. By first calling the Frisbee the Pluto Platter, Wham-O tapped into America's fascination at the time with UFOs.

With demonstrations and giveaways, Wham-O stirred up wild interest in its hula

Fad Toys:

Classic toys invented in California have been fun for a long time.

hoop in 1958. The introduction of the hula hoop represents the greatest toy fad ever—25 million were sold in the first 4 months.

These toys are more than passing whims, however. They have lasted well beyond their initial craze.

The spin on yo-yos is given at California's National Yo-Yo Museum in Chico (320 Broadway; 530–893–0545). The museum traces the history of the yo-yo and also displays one giant example—the world's largest wooden yo-yo at 265 pounds, 50 inches in diameter.

The Frisbee has been spun into several popular sports, including ultimate Frisbee and Frisbee golf, invented in California in 1977 by the man who patented the disk's modern design, Ed Headrick.

you know you're in
california when...
...you're surrounded by fruits and nuts

Just try to go through a day without eating something from California. California produces almost every single morsel grown in this country of several different crops, including almonds, artichokes, kiwifruit, olives, raisins, and walnuts.

More than America's breadbasket, California is also its crisper. In fact, why not throw in the whole fridge, kitchen, and pantry, too.

California is easily the country's number-one agricultural producer, annually harvesting more than 350 different crops—everything from persimmons to pistachios. Agriculture is a $25-billion industry that accounts for 10 percent of the state's employment.

And let's not forget dairy either, where the state is the nation's number-one producer as well.

Probably California's signature fruit is the avocado, with most of the crop grown in San Diego County. There you'll find Fallbrook, home of—you guessed it—the Avocado Festival.

Fallbrook's festival is probably the only event in the world that includes competitive avocado racing. Unlike NASCAR events, crashes in these races end up with something positive—good-tasting guacamole.

Farming:

California produces a lot of good things to eat.

Many other towns take time to celebrate their bounty at harvest time, with dozens of fruit and vegetable festivals on the table throughout the year. Notable events include fetes to garlic in Gilroy, eggplants in Loomis, dates in Indio, and carrots—yes carrots—in Holtville.

The tiny town of Castroville always has something to stalk about—its annual Artichoke Festival. In 1947, Marilyn Monroe, then an unknown Norma Jean, was crowned the festival's first artichoke queen, to show that people in California aren't so "nutty" after all.

you know you're in
california when...

...almost everyone makes a pitch

Welcome to Hollywood, where appearances can be deceiving. Your waitress? A wannabe starlet. The guy driving your taxi? He's got a sure blockbuster screenplay in the glove box, if only someone would green-light his project.

Yes, the lure of Hollywood is powerful indeed. The movie industry is a driving force in California, and that's why people keep driving to California with dreams of fame and fortune.

It has been this way since the early 1900s, when eastern movie companies headed west to set up shop in Hollywood. The draw back then was good light and great weather, allowing for year-round outdoor shooting.

The first movie filmed entirely in California was shot in 1908. Reels and reels of footage have been shot and edited here ever since.

Nowadays Hollywood is a film capital in name only. While the movie industry still has a strong presence in Southern California, only one major studio, Paramount, remains in Hollywood.

Visitors can still capture some of the past glamour by stepping on Hollywood Boulevard's Walk of Fame, sidewalk plaques dedicated to famous entertainers.

The opulent Kodak Theater, located at the intersection of Hollywood Boulevard and Highland Avenue, anchors a new retail complex and puts some of the shine back in Hollywood's former glitter. The theater also returned to Hollywood the film industry's biggest party, the Academy Awards ceremony.

A great introduction to the movie business is the Hollywood Entertainment Museum (7021 Hollywood Boulevard; 323–465–7900; www.hollywoodmuseum.com). The museum offers a behind-the-scenes look at the history of moviemaking and the Hollywood community. It also features an incredibly detailed miniature representation of Hollywood as it looked in the 1940s, featuring 45 city blocks and 450 small-scale buildings.

Studios offering tours include Sony Pictures (323–520–8687; Culver City) and Universal (800–864–8377; Universal City). Smile as you walk around—you might be discovered.

Film Industry:

Filmmaking plays a starring role in California.

you know you're in
california when...
...the Russians have come and gone

If the Russians who invaded California in 1812 were better at farming, who knows how world history would have turned out.

The Russians were coming to set up a military outpost in Northern California with an eye toward expansion to the east and south. A government-sponsored company built a well-protected fort and a surrounding village. Settlers included Russians and native Alaskans who began hunting sea otters, planting crops, and raising cattle.

In a relatively short time the Russians defeated themselves by over-hunting the sea otters and failing miserably at agriculture. The fort was abandoned in 1839 and the Russians retreated from plans of dominating North America.

The Russians called their California settlement Fort Ross, a shortened form of *Rossiya*, the name at the time of their motherland. The Russians also called the nearby river *Slavyanka*, After they left that was changed by Californians to the more easily pronounced Russian River.

Fort Ross was eventually taken over by the state as a historic landmark, and it is now open as a state park. It's located 12 miles north of Jenner on Highway 1 (707–847–3286).

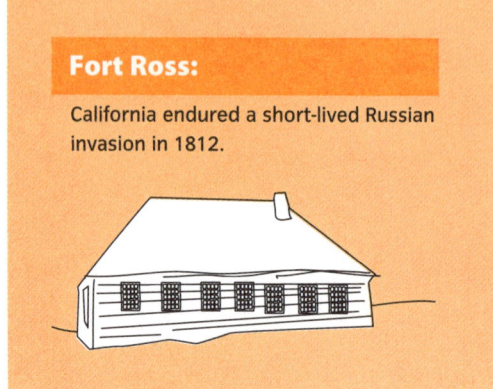

Fort Ross:

California endured a short-lived Russian invasion in 1812.

Visitors can wander about and imagine what life was like at this Russian fort of the early 19th century. Or envision what it was like to be a prisoner then, as the grounds include a stockade.

The park also features reconstructed barracks, two corner block houses with cannons, and the Rotchev House, the only original building on the site. The latter was made in 1836 for Alexander Rotchev, the last Russian manager at Fort Ross. It's the oldest house north of San Francisco.

you know you're in
california when...
...freeways are a way of life

Ah, California freeways, glorious ribbons of asphalt that zip you from one place to another.... Well, not exactly. If you travel at 3:00 A.M., maybe you zip along.

Otherwise, as Californians know, freeways are never free of choking traffic. Some, like the San Diego Freeway, are actually long parking lots for most of the day, a sea of brake lights and simmering road rage.

In California there is no escaping the freeway, a fixture here since 1940. In that year California opened the nation's first freeway, the Arroyo Seco Parkway, which connected downtown Los Angeles with Pasadena.

Pennsylvanians might squawk that a turnpike that opened in the Keystone State a few months earlier was actually the nation's first freeway. But that was a toll road and hence not free. Case closed.

The Arroyo Seco, now named the Pasadena Freeway, thrilled motorists when it first opened, but now it often provides unwanted thrills. It features banked turns and offers no turnout lanes for motorists in trouble. Entering the Pasadena at some points requires drivers to simulate drag racing, as they must accelerate from a standing stop to freeway pace in a matter of a few yards. This is the state's scariest high-speed ride outside an amusement park.

Traveling along the thousands of miles of other California freeways, while often slow, is usually safer. Some freeway interchanges are architectural wonders, with four levels of connecting lanes.

Californians refer to freeways by their travel direction, as in "I'll take the Hollywood" (101 Freeway), or "I'll take the Santa Monica" (10 Freeway), or simply a catch-all phrase, as in "I'll take the freeway."

Which freeway to take is based on whether there is a "Sig Alert"—a California term for a traffic tie-up. A Sig Alert is named after Loyd Sigmon, a radio engineer who rigged a system that allowed Los Angeles police officers to signal radio stations whenever there were road emergencies to broadcast. The first one aired in 1955.

Freeways:

California freeways take you everywhere, but sometimes very slowly.

you know you're in
california when...
...history has a golden thread

It took one word to make California a state. Of course, it was a pretty loaded word, and one that was often shouted in moments of frenzied glee.

Gold. That was it. Before gold was discovered in 1848, California was a sleepy region with a few thousand folks and nice weather. Then John Marshall spotted some flickering yellow in the American River, and before you could say "Eureka!" California became a state with close to a quarter-million residents.

Gold Rush. Gold Fever. Marshall's discovery sure made people crazy. Thousands dropped whatever they were doing and headed west with shovels, gold pans, and dreams of a mother lode.

Most neglected to read the fine print. Most of the easy gold was gone early in the rush. Life in a mining town was primitive, and gold mining was hard work. In all, 125 million ounces of gold were taken from California's hills in the fifty years after Marshall's discovery, but few people got rich. Marshall himself died a pauper.

California's nickname, the Golden State, is a lasting reminder of its Gold Rush days. You can find a lot of this history along Highway 49 in California's Gold Country.

The Empire Mine Historic Park in Grass Valley (530–273–8522) offers exhibits and historic structures that show the gritty life of hard-rock miners. Malakoff Diggins State Historic Park in North Bloomfield was the site of one of the most destructive methods of mining. Here water cannons blasted away hillsides in a frantic search for gold.

You can go right to the source and visit the John Marshall Gold Discovery State Park in Coloma (530–622–3470), The park includes a replica of Sutter's Mill, where Marshall made his discovery. Rent or buy equipment here and go mining yourself in the nearby river.

This is probably a good time to mention that most of California's gold remains undiscovered.

Gold Rush:
John Marshall's discovery of gold was a pivotal event in California's history.

EUREKA!

you know you're in
california when...
...the color gold looks a lot like orange

The Golden Gate Bridge is such a majestic landmark that it would be foolish to quibble about the fact that it's not really golden at all. The bridge's name comes from the waters that it spans: the Golden Gate Straight.

According to bridge officials, the color of the Golden Gate is orange vermilion, which sounds a lot fancier than just plain orange.

When the Golden Gate was built, the U.S. Navy requested that the bridge be painted in garish black-and-yellow stripes to make it more visible to passing ships in the fog. Millions of tourists who have made the bridge a gorgeous centerpiece of their souvenir photographs can be thankful that the Navy's request was turned down.

The Golden Gate, connecting San Francisco with Marin County, opened May 28, 1937. About forty million cars cross it each year. Stunning views of the city, the Marin Headlands, and the glimmering Pacific make this a magical journey. Just try to keep your eyes on the road. Many others either walk or bike across—great fun too, if you don't mind a little wind in your face.

The Golden Gate's distinctive hue has generated myths about how its exterior is maintained. Rumors have long circulated that painters begin at one end, and by the time they get to the other side it's time to start from the beginning. Not true. The bridge receives regular touch-ups as needed.

The Golden Gate's appealing tint may be one reason it has garnered more publicity than its nearby steel cousin, the San Francisco–Oakland Bay Bridge. The Bay Bridge was completed several months before the Golden Gate, is equally impressive in construction, and is twice as long. But it's painted gray. Advantage, Golden Gate.

While you may not be able to build your own Golden Gate Bridge at home, you can duplicate its color. Bridge officials have revealed that it's known as PMS 173.

> **Golden Gate Bridge:**
> This structure is a ridiculously scenic span that connects San Francisco with Marin County.

you know you're in
california when...
...bears are everywhere

The California grizzly bear *(Ursus californicus)* is widely seen throughout the state, but only in a symbolic sense.

Thousands of California grizzlies once roamed freely along the state's coast and low-mountain areas. Then settlers hunted them all down. The last grizzly bear in California was killed in Tulare County in 1922.

California grizzlies finally got some love and respect when they were adopted as the official state animal in 1953.

The grizzly is a wisely chosen state symbol. Grizzlies have many admirable qualities. They are big, powerful creatures that dominate the food chain. They lead a desirable lifestyle that includes frequent travel, lots of eating, some mating, and long winter vacations. Like so many Californians, they are often playful and enjoy salmon.

The California grizzly is featured prominently on the state flag and state seal. In more unofficial ways the grizzly has been used as a California symbol on items ranging from food labels to political cartoons. A cuddly bear is the mascot of the University of California at Berkeley.

California's bear flag is based on a design created by settlers who took over a Mexican garrison in Sonoma in 1846. They needed to quickly raise a banner to declare independence from Mexico. Their flag, with

Grizzly Bear:

Californians cherish the grizzly as an important state symbol, even though you have to leave the state to find a real one.

a five-pointed red star and the image of a small bear, was so hastily made that some people thought the bear resembled a pig.

That confusion was cleared up with the introduction of California's official state flag, adopted in 1911. That flag features a big-shouldered grizzly lumbering across a grassy mound with its head tilted slightly toward the viewer, flashing a kind of "What are you looking at?" glare. Now that's an image a state can rally around.

you know you're in
california when...
...you fish with your bare hands

Pity the poor grunion fish. Coming ashore to make love, it may well end up in a frying pan, lightly covered with batter.

Southern California's annual grunion hunt is probably the wackiest outdoor sport in the world. It's loads of fun for people, but not for the grunion, a pesky, 6-inch silvery fish with peculiar mating habits.

During the spring and summer months, grunion come ashore in droves to mate along Southern California beaches. No other fish on the planet leaves the ocean to mate—which makes sense, since fish belong in the ocean. The grunion's mating ritual involves frenzied land movements you'll never see any other fish attempt.

The action begins close to midnight during grunion season, on days when the tide is just right. It all happens in a flash. The grunion catch waves and land on the wet sand, where the females drills themselves into a hole with their heads sticking straight up. Yes, it's just as weird-looking as it sounds.

Each female lays hundreds of eggs in the sand, which are immediately fertilized by several males who curl around her. Then all the fish dash back into the sea.

That is, if they make it. Those frenzied seconds of mating are the time when grunion hunters strike, if they can. You see, by law grunion must be captured by hand. And, well, they're pretty slippery and determined to return to the water.

Because the grunion's sexual antics are closely tied to moon phases and tidal changes, grunion experts can predict what nights the amorous fish will appear. You can visit the California Department of Fish and Game's Web site (www.dfg.ca.gov) for the annual grunion schedule.

Grunion got their name from the Spanish word for *grunter*, since the fish make a squeaking noise during mating. But it also stands for the sound most people emit as they bend over and make mostly futile attempts to grab a handful of grunion.

Grunion Fishing:

During grunion season, Southern Californians hold beach parties as they wait for the elusive silvery fish to appear.

you know you're in
california when...
...you wear flowers in your hair

Back in the late 1960s it seemed that every young American was donning tie-dyed clothing, piling into VW vans plastered with peace stickers, and heading to ground zero of America's counterculture movement, the intersection of Haight and Ashbury Streets in San Francisco.

The Haight was as good a place as any to "turn on, tune in, and drop out," as Timothy Leary urged this restless generation to do. There were cheap crash pads, plenty of groovy folk, and exciting events such as the Human Be-In at nearby Golden Gate Park in 1967, the year that ushered in the Summer of Love.

Another attraction was the Haight's vibrant music scene, which included legendary local talent such as the Grateful Dead, Jefferson Airplane, and Janis Joplin.

The times have certainly a-changed for the former hippie enclave. The Grateful Dead are long gone from the area, and the closest thing you'll get to them now is a Cherry Garcia ice cream cone at the Ben & Jerry's located at the intersection of Haight and Ashbury. The Dead's flophouse from the 1960s still draws visitors at 710 Ashbury Street.

Businesses such as the People's Cafe (1419 Haight Street; 415–553–8842) and the Bound Together Anarchist Collective Bookstore (1369 Haight Street; 415–431–8355) pay tribute to the neighborhood's counterculture roots.

The Haight-Ashbury Free Clinic (415–552–2114; www.hafci.org), which opened in 1967 near the corner of Haight and Clayton, thrives today. The Red Victorian Movie House (1727 Haight Street; 415–668–3944; www.redvicmoviehouse.com) still offers funky seating in the form of big, comfy couches.

But trendier, more upscale boutiques dominate the area, even though one or two head shops remain, harkening back to an earlier time of pipe-dream bliss.

Those seeking a more current counterculture zone in California should head to the hills— the volcanic Mount Shasta region in the state's northern zone, where a hippie mentality lives on. Some even believe a mysterious troop of telepaths known as Lumerians live here too.

Haight-Ashbury:

This San Francisco neighborhood embraced California's counterculture heritage during the 1960s.

you know you're in california when...

...writers shine a light on some dark places

The genre of hard-boiled detective fiction was born and perfected in California, a place that most people see as sunny-side up. A few great writers probed beneath the state's glittery surface to reveal a more sordid world of tough-guy criminals and even grittier heroes out to catch them.

Dashiell Hammett introduced this new style of crime writing when he published *The Maltese Falcon* in 1930, introducing his detective hero Sam Spade. Hammett had worked as a detective in San Francisco during the 1920s, so when he wrote about a city of swindling dames, scheming blackmailers, and assorted thieves, he knew his material.

Raymond Chandler picked up the smoking gun after Hammett and created his own dark crime world based in Los Angeles. Chandler penned such noir classics as *The Big Sleep, Farewell, My Lovely,* and *The Long Goodbye*.

Chandler's Los Angeles, with its lurid crimes, hard-nosed gamblers, and crooked cops, wasn't chamber-of-commerce material. Still, he is honored in Los Angeles at the intersection of Hollywood and Cahuenga Boulevards. The spot is designated Raymond Chandler Square; it is the site of the office of Chandler's fictional detective hero, Philip Marlowe.

Hard-Boiled Detective Fiction:

Crime isn't pretty in classic crime novels set in California.

The scenic beauty of Santa Barbara didn't fool Kenneth Millar, who continued the hard-boiled efforts begun by Hammett and Chandler with his own brand of crime fiction that he wrote while living there. Millar used the pen name Ross Macdonald to publish many classic detective novels between 1949 and 1976. The novels were set in Southern California and featured his fictional private eye, Lew Archer.

Meanwhile, in Ventura, just south of Santa Barbara, Erle Stanley Gardner set up shop as an attorney and then turned to crime writing and created his hero, Perry Mason.

It would be a crime if you didn't read one of these great California detective fiction writers.

you know you're in
california when...
...one man's house really was his castle

When you lived life as large as William Randolph Hearst, you needed a really large place to live. His 90,000-square-foot primary residence in San Simeon reflected his expansive ego and immense sphere of influence in 20th-century America.

Hearst was a publishing, broadcast, and Hollywood tycoon who dabbled in politics and relished his power to influence public opinion. His estate, known as Hearst Castle, was equally imposing.

Hearst contacted San Francisco architect Julia Morgan in 1919 when the extensive property consisted only of camping tents. Hearst envisioned a more permanent residence, writing Morgan that he wanted to "build a little something." It boggles the mind to think what he would have considered a "big something."

The colossal estate included 56 bedrooms, 41 fireplaces, a landing strip, 127 acres of gardens, 3 lavishly decorated pools, and enough paintings and antiquities to fill several museums.

Exotic animals such as yaks, llamas, camels, and zebras grazed the hillsides of the property, so incoming guests were treated to a spectacle even before they arrived at the front door.

With a well-stocked wine cellar, this was clearly one dynamic place to party.

Assorted VIPs, ranging from Charlie Chaplin to Winston Churchill, dropped by for elaborate bashes.

By 1947 dwindling finances and declining health forced Hearst to move out. After he died, the property was deeded to the state. It's now a state historic monument open for guided tours (800–444–4445).

Keep your eyes peeled on the way in, as zebras are still spotted wandering about the grounds.

Hearst Castle:
This colossal California palace is a tribute to William Randolph Hearst's grand lifestyle.

you know you're in
california when...
...you've got brains and looks

True, superficial pursuits like maintaining a well-buffed body are a priority among Californians, more so than most Americans. But that doesn't mean Californians neglect to give their brains a workout, too.

California offers its residents a state-of-the art gymnasium of the mind, a three-tiered college and university program that is the biggest and arguably the best public higher education system in the world.

So just erase that caricature of your typical Californian as an airhead. There's plenty of deep thinking going on at public campuses across the state, starting with what Californians know as the "UC" or the University of California.

The UC features ten sites, from the esteemed original Berkeley campus to its newest site at Merced, and including scenic coastal spots such as UC Santa Barbara and UC Santa Cruz. UC students learn from some of the top minds in the country, including more Nobel Prize Laureates than at any other university in the world.

If a student can't make it to a UC school they can opt for a CSU, or a California State University. This second-tier system, with 23 campuses and 400,000 students, is the largest public university in the world.

Higher Education:

California's public college and university system is at the head of the class.

Some degree-seekers complete their first two years of higher education at one of the state's 109 community colleges, where an entire year of classes costs only a few hundred bucks, or roughly the price of one science textbook. Then they transfer to a UC to get a four-year degree, thereby saving two years of high tuition costs worth thousands of dollars. Now, that's showing some brains.

you know you're in
california when...
...driving has many ups and downs

In San Francisco, with some of the world's steepest hills, driving is not really about getting from one place to another but more like competing in an extreme sport.

As you crest one of the city's precipitous inclines, with the front of the car pointed skyward, you'll feel as if you're ready for launch. During roller coaster-like descents, you'll have your foot clamped hard on the brake pedal, your stomach tied in knots.

San Francisco has more than forty hills, and we're not talking wimpy mounds. Streets such as Filbert between Hyde and Leavenworth have grades of more than 30 percent. To add to the challenge, the city's steepest hills all have stop signs at their highest point. This gives you a moment's pause to consider your precarious situation before taking your foot off the brake pedal and making a frantic lurch over the top, praying you don't roll back and uncertain of what lies ahead.

Yes, San Francisco driving is the ultimate test of nerves behind the wheel, and a critical challenge for anyone daring to pass through the city in a manual-transmission vehicle.

In the 1920s city officials designed a section of Lombard Street with eight switchbacks intended to make it easier to descend the block's steep grade. It worked, but Lombard's hairpin turns have lured thrill seekers to what is now billed as a major tourist attraction, the "Crookedest Street in the World."

This corkscrew section of Lombard is between Hyde and Leavenworth Streets. Drivers line up to descend the flower-lined lane at turtle-like speeds of 5 mph. At the bottom of the hill, dozens of tourists snap away to photograph the spectacle.

In 1968 filmmakers took advantage of San Francisco's hilly streets to record one of the best car movie chase scenes ever in *Bullitt*. It doesn't take movie magic to re-create the buzz for any driver—the city's streets are exciting enough as they are.

The (Hilly) Streets of San Francisco:

Driving this city's steep hills is not for those with weak hearts or faulty brakes.

you know you're in
california when...
...meal planning and music are a great duet

Picking a concert to attend at the Hollywood Bowl is easy. The real challenge is figuring out what to bring to eat before the music starts.

Anyone who buys a concert ticket sets in motion elaborate planning for that all-important pre-concert picnic at the Bowl, a venerable Los Angeles tradition. For many Bowl patrons the musical agenda is of secondary concern to what's on the dinner menu.

Before a note is played, there are platefuls of lip-smacking food to consume and plenty of beverages to drink. The Bowl opens four hours before each concert to accommodate the many picnics being spread. Some Bowl regulars pack elaborate mobile feasts in a seeming competition to outdo fellow picnickers.

Box seating close to the stage provides a plush *al fresco* dining experience, while picnic tables and grassy spots farther out offer a more rustic alternative.

Eating aside, this is one great place to hear music. The Bowl is the largest natural amphitheater in the world.

The first Bowl concert was held in 1922, with simple wooden benches perched on the hillside. Permanent improvements have been added since, including a modern band shell installed before the 2004 season that features improved acoustics, video cameras, large viewing screens, and even a fireworks launching pad.

Performers here have ranged from Pavarotti to Pink Floyd, from the Beatles to Billie Holiday. The Bowl (2301 North Highland Avenue; 323–850–2000; www.hollywoodbowl.com) is the summer home of the Los Angeles Philharmonic and year-round location for its resident ensemble, the Hollywood Bowl Orchestra.

Hollywood Bowl:

Angelenos believe the Bowl's natural acoustics were dampened considerably by construction of the Hollywood Freeway during the 1950s.

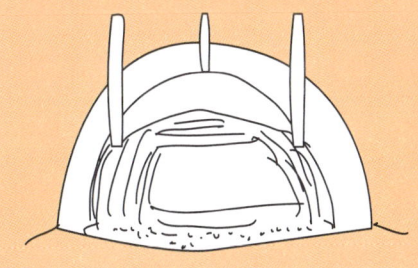

you know you're in
california when...
...nine letters have star power

They are just nine white block letters perched on a hill. That's it. Somehow they've become one of the world's most recognized landmarks.

Sure, it helps that the letters spell out *Hollywood*. For many, this steel sign captures the glamour and excitement of the movie industry. Awestruck tourists have snapped millions of pictures of it, making it the world's most photographed sign.

The sign's potent symbolism wasn't reflected in its original purpose. It was built in 1923 to point the way to a new housing development in the Hollywood Hills. It was lit up by hundreds of lights and spelled *Hollywoodland*, the name of the new subdivision.

Once the housing development was fully sold, the sign was abandoned like a fading movie star, and it fell into disrepair. It was turned over to Los Angeles during World War II and the "land" letters were removed.

The sign was refurbished in the 1970s, when it regained its luster. It has been watched over by the Hollywood Chamber of Commerce ever since.

Getting to the sign, just like breaking into Hollywood, is difficult. In fact, it is illegal to hike to the sign from the Hollywood Hills, even though many people do it anyway.

Hollywood Sign:

The letters that spell out Hollywood near the peak of Mt. Lee are 45 feet high.

Rangers in Griffith Park, which houses the sign, keep a watch out for trespassers.

The heavy surveillance hasn't deterred pranksters from adding comic twists to the sign's lettering. For example, the sign was changed to read "Hollyweed" in the 1970s after the state passed a new marijuana law, and to "Ollywood" during the Iran-Contra hearings.

you know you're in
california when...
...all eyes are on the finish line

Horse racing is one of your riskier investments. That's why you scratch your head at Californians, who turned in a big way to gambling on horses during the Great Depression, when the state's five major thoroughbred tracks first opened.

Since then, Californians have wagered billions of hard-earned dollars on the likelihood of a powerful, unpredictable animal being first to reach the finish line. California is the country's biggest market for horse racing, with enough money wagered at California tracks to fund a small country—sometimes in a single day.

The Del Mar racetrack north of San Diego (858–755–1141; www.dmtc.com), for example, set a track record by collecting more than $24 million in bets in one day.

Hollywood crooner Bing Crosby first lured racing fans to Del Mar in 1937 with a catchy jingle about the beautiful track "where the surf meets the turf." This is a glamour track, where patrons arrive in high fashion toting thick wallets to a fabled track with an ocean view and Spanish colonial–style architecture.

The California racing scene includes Santa Anita in Arcadia (626–574–7223; www.santaanita.com), which opened in 1934, and Hollywood Park in Inglewood (310–419–1500; www.hollywoodpark.com), dating from 1938. There's more wagering in Northern California at Golden Gate Fields in Berkeley (510–559–7300; www.goldengatefields.com), which opened in 1941, and in San Mateo at Bay Meadows (650–574–7223; www.baymeadows.com), which held its first race in 1934.

Califonia's most celebrated thoroughbred was Seabiscuit, a knobby-kneed but gritty racer who became a national hero. Seabiscuit boosted the reputation of California racing when he won a dramatic match race against eastern power War Admiral in 1938, a contest dubbed "the match of the century."

After his stellar career, Seabiscuit retired to Ridgewood Ranch in Northern California near Willits, where he was visited by legions of fans during his stud years. He was buried there in 1947. You can tour the ranch (707–459–5992) and see Seabiscuit's barn and other remaining structures.

Horse Racing:
The sport of kings gets the royal treatment in California.

you know you're in
california when...
...computers learn to talk to each other

It would be stretching it to say that the Internet was invented in California. Just ask Al Gore about the folly of making claims like that. But it's clear that the Internet took its first baby steps in California.

Before there were millions of computers connected to the data network we now know as the Internet, there were just two. And they were in California.

One was at UCLA in Westwood and the other at the Stanford Research Institute in Menlo Park. These computers were operated by technology whizzes developing a network to exchange data.

The first successful message between these two network "nodes" isn't etched in memory along the lines of other big moments in communication history, such as the "Watson, come here. I need you!" spoken at the birth of the telephone.

No, the first Internet message wasn't even a word. It was the letter *l*. It was typed at UCLA on October 29, 1969, and soon after a reply came from Menlo Park: "Got the *l*." That was the birth of the Internet.

Never mind that those computer geeks were hoping to type in the word *login* and the system crashed when they got to the letter *g*. It all worked soon enough.

This first data network was called the ARPANET, part of a government project funded to develop better American computer skills. Creating a data network was a big part of the plan.

One of the leaders in getting the ARPANET to work was UCLA faculty member Leonard Kleinrock. He helped shape the early technology that has led to the Internet's key attributes of being a shared network that is always on.

Later, a third node was added to this network at UC Santa Barbara. The ARPANET paved the way for the Internet, and eventually for e-mail and the World Wide Web, and there's no need to say how important they've become.

The Internet:

The first time two computers talked with each other over a data network happened in California.

you know you're in
california when...
...you're all jazzed up

To hear some of the world's best jazz music in California, you don't have to head to a smoke-filled nightclub late at night. You can spread a blanket under a canopy of oak trees. In broad daylight. Really. And maybe catch an ocean swim or a round of golf in between performances.

The venerable Monterey Jazz Festival has been held since 1958 at the Monterey County Fairgrounds (831–372–5863; www.montereycountyfair.com), a lush setting more appropriate for, well, a fair, not for red-hot jazz sets. While there is a fair here every summer, the focus then turns to jazz music in September.

The first Monterey Jazz Festival (www.montereyjazzfestival.org) kicked off with legendary trumpeter Dizzy Gillespie puffing out his cheeks to blow the *Star Spangled Banner*. Later, singer Billie Holiday gave one of her final performances. Organizers of the event say it is the longest-running jazz festival in the world.

Jazz sounds were heard in California long before the first Monterey festival. A blazing jazz scene was located along Central Avenue in Los Angeles from the 1920s through the 1950s. Performers included Louis Armstrong, Jelly Roll Morton, and Duke Ellington.

Jazz:

California was quick to get on the jazz bandwagon and has kept the beat alive.

After that, the scene shifted to the Lighthouse Cafe in Hermosa Beach and a cooler musical style known as West Coast jazz, featuring artists such as Gerry Mulligan and Chet Baker.

During its jazz heyday, the Lighthouse (30 Pier Avenue; 310–376–9833; www.thelighthousecafe.net) was famous for its marathon jam sessions. Now the club features a lineup of rock and blues music but occasionally hosts a special tribute to its West Coast jazz roots.

you know you're in
california when...

...you look like a cowboy but you've never been on a horse

Probably no other pants evoke the spirit of the American West like blue jeans. Strap on a pair of jeans and you immediately feel more rugged and pioneering. Rebellious, even.

American blue jeans trace their roots to the Gold Rush days of San Francisco and the efforts of Levi Strauss and Jacob Davis.

Strauss was a Bavarian immigrant who arrived in San Francisco in 1853 to open a dry goods business. Davis was a tailor who showed Strauss a clever way to use rivets to make denim pants more resilient. In 1873 they patented this rivet system for making "waist overalls," and blue jeans were born.

One of the most interesting tidbits of this history is that Strauss's first name, now synonymous with jeans, originally was Loeb, which would be a funny name to call jeans, as in: "It's a casual party, right? I'll just wear my Loebs." Thankfully Strauss had changed his first name by the time he arrived in America.

Jeans were a hit with workers and eventually went mainstream in the early twentieth century, popularized by the many Levi's-clad cowboys appearing in westerns. The rest is apparel history, as Levi jeans remain an enduring American symbol, much more than just pants.

Jeans:

San Francisco's two clothing kings, Levi's and the Gap, have intertwining histories and a big say in what Americans wear.

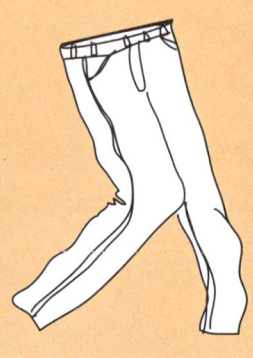

Levi's jeans are linked to another San Francisco clothing giant, the Gap. The Gap chain began in 1969, when Doris and Don Fisher opened their first store in San Francisco with the intention of making it easier to buy Levi's jeans. The store name was a play on the term *generation gap,* a phrase much uttered during that socially turbulent year of Woodstock.

Today the Gap is very much a part of the establishment as a major company that includes Banana Republic and Old Navy.

you know you're in
california when...
...you reach for the stars

In the early 20th century, space travel was just science fiction. Then a group of particularly brainy people in Pasadena turned rocket science into a reality.

Calling themselves the Jet Propulsion Laboratory (JPL), this team of high-flyers launched a test rocket in 1936 from a dry riverbed near the Rose Bowl. Eventually they fired their first unguided missile, which soared 7 miles into the air.

Laugh all you want at their pocket-protector fashion. The geeks at JPL really know how to zoom into space. Managed by the California Institute of Technology for the National Aeronautics and Space Administration, JPL has been at the forefront of America's space exploration for decades.

JPL created and managed America's first satellite, Explorer I, launched in 1958, quickly getting the United States up to speed with their chief space rival, the Soviet Union. JPL sent the first robotic crafts to the moon, paving the way for the historic Apollo lunar landing in 1969.

As the Apollo astronauts were touching down on the moon, JPL was already sending other unmanned craft to Mars and beyond. JPL has also turned its equipment on our own planet in an effort to better understand life on Earth. For a kick, why not probe *them*? They offer tours (818–354–4321).

While most of us are proud of our vacation photos, nothing compares to the snapshots JPL produces from its far-flung journeys. Its roving crafts have sent back thousands of pictures of conditions on other planets in our solar system, and even produced a "group portrait" of the system in the early 1990s.

Jet Propulsion Laboratory:

These rocket scientists are on a mission to understand the universe and beyond.

you know you're in
california when...
...a peculiar tree grows in the desert

In a world where nature was admired only for its beauty, Joshua trees wouldn't get any respect. They are anything but stately. No, not with trunks that look like strands of dried-out spaghetti, and limbs formed in grotesque, twisted shapes that more or less point skyward.

It is as if the trees were pleading with the heavens to be struck down by lightning and put out of their misery.

California explorer John Fremont called them "the most repulsive tree in the vegetable kingdom." Ouch. Yet Californians have a soft spot in their hearts for these tortured trees, whose horrid forms reflect a fierce battle for survival against the elements. Like loveable underdogs, Joshua trees are adored symbols of California's deserts.

They are mostly found in the protected area that bears their name, the Joshua Tree National Park (760–367–5500), nearly 800,000 acres of desert landscape in the state's southern region just east of Palm Springs. It is a harsh climate that appears mostly dormant, but, especially after a rainfall, springs to life with surprising splashes of color and beauty. Even the Joshua trees sprout creamy white blossoms on their spiny leaves, mostly in late winter and early spring.

The park, with great examples of high and low desert environments, is a favorite of people seeking the nurturing serenity of the desert. The National Park Service describes Joshua Tree as a "refuge for the human spirit." It is also a great place for hiking, with almost 200 miles of trails, and a favorite spot for rock climbers as well.

Joshua Tree was first declared a national monument in 1936, thanks in part to the efforts of Pasadena socialite Minerva Hoyt, who decried the practice of poachers who were raiding desert areas and hauling back assorted vegetation for their own gardens. The area became a national park in 1994.

Joshua Trees:

Mormon pioneers named them because the trees' outstretched limbs reminded them of Joshua leading the Israelites to the Promised Land.

you know you're in
california when...
...a town is sweet to its core

Sure, a fine crust is vital to baking a great apple pie. To state the obvious, however, the most important ingredient in an apple pie is, duh, the apples.

That's what makes the quaint mountain town of Julian a prime attraction, at least when it comes to apple pie. It's the apples.

Julian is just one great place to grow apples. People here tell you it has something to do with the area's climate, soil, minerals, and elevation. They grow them all up here—from pippins and McIntosh to more exotic varieties such as Northern Spy and Arkansas Black.

In the fall thousands of apples are harvested and sent into town to be peeled, cored, and prepared as filling for pies baked by several local shops. The sweet aroma wafting through Julian's historic downtown draws thousands of visitors looking for a slice of heaven.

Some apples are pressed into fresh cider, another major temptation sold around town. You can also eat the pure apple, and even pick your own at some local orchards.

The town's initial lure wasn't apples, but rather gold. An 1869 discovery of gold in a creek here sent miners racing to Julian in what was the San Diego area's only gold rush.

Julian Apple Pies:
Everyone saves room for dessert during apple harvest time in Julian.

When the rush subsided, many miners stayed on and sought their fortune not in gold but in golden delicious and other varieties of apples. Town founders suspected that there was something special about their apples, and those suspicions were confirmed when Julian apples won a taste competition at the Chicago World's Fair in 1893.

The best time to visit is the fall, when downtown shops use locally grown apples to make their fresh-baked pies. During the rest of the year, out-of-town apples are brought in to do the job, but the pies still taste pretty good.

you know you're in california when...
...things are hopping

When Mark Twain wrote a short story in 1865 about an amazing jumping frog from Calaveras County, he was only kidding. Somehow, though, Twain's tall tale has been spun into a real-life event, the biggest occasion on the social calendar in these parts.

With a wink toward readers, Twain claimed his work, "The Celebrated Jumping Frog of Calaveras County," was based on a story he had heard at a local tavern while he was visiting the area during the Gold Rush. In the story a great leaping frog named Dan'l Webster loses a jumping contest when a cheater crams the frog's stomach with buckshot.

Seizing on the popularity of the story, Calaveras County officials launched the Frog Jumping Jubilee in 1928. The contest has been a central event at the county's annual fair ever since.

The frog-jumping contest is held every year on the third weekend in May during the Calaveras County Fair (209–736–2561; www.frogtown.org). It draws hundreds of hopping-mad contestants who compete to see which croaking leaper can jump the farthest.

The world's record was set in 1986 by Rosie the Ribeter at 21 feet and 5¾ inches. That earned Rosie a revered spot in the Frog Hop of Fame, plaques embedded in the sidewalk of downtown Angels Camp to honor past victors. This is clearly one frog-friendly town.

Frogs are coached by human jockeys, who sometimes scoop them up from local ponds a day or so before the event, hoping to keep their legs fresh. Others can rent frogs to join in the fun.

Other activities at the fair include a rodeo, livestock auction, parades, music, crafts, food, and a beauty pageant. Forget the plaque—maybe the winning frog should get a chance at kissing the pageant beauty to see what happens.

Jumping Frog Jubilee:
California hosts the world's most celebrated frog jumping contest.

you know you're in
california when...
...digging through muck is a learning experience

The idea that balmy L.A. was once a frosty environment without the aid of air conditioning seems laughable today. But the cold facts lie in the oozing pools of an area known as the La Brea Tar Pits.

In this mess scientists have unearthed the world's greatest collection of Ice Age plant and animal fossils.

Between 10,000 and 40,000 years ago, underground asphalt rose to the surface and trapped thousands of unfortunate animals and plants. Then the natural slime did modern scientists a favor by neatly protecting the remains for future discovery.

Excavations were begun here in the early twentieth century. So far, more than three million artifacts have been recovered at the site, including one million bones.

The collection is displayed at the on-site Page Museum (5801 Wilshire Boulevard; 323–934–7243). The discoveries reveal a precise portrait of Ice Age Los Angeles. In short, it appears to have been one big feeding frenzy, a kind of dog-eat-ground-sloth world.

Once an animal—say, a mammoth or a saber-toothed cat—was trapped in the sticky tar, various predators jumped in for the potential feast, only to be trapped themselves. One of the most common finds here is the remains of the dire wolf.

The digging continues. In the summer visitors can watch the work at Pit 91 on the museum grounds. Inside the museum visitors can peer into a glass-walled laboratory and observe white-coated workers clean and catalog new finds, a tedious and seemingly endless task.

Meanwhile, sticky pools of asphalt surrounding the museum are hard at work, too, bubbling away and trapping modern-day victims such as pigeons, rodents, and even dogs.

La Brea Tar Pits:

A gooey excavation site that has yielded an amazing fossil collection.

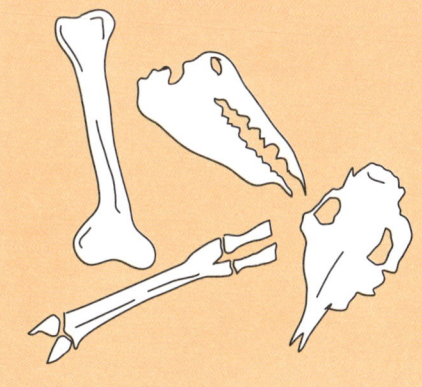

you know you're in
california when...
...an international crossing is a snap

The lure of another country only a short car ride away is too strong to resist for Californians. More than 300,000 people travel each day between the Mexican border town of Tijuana and San Ysidro, California, making it the world's busiest international crossing.

Tijuana may be touristy and not as genuine as other parts of Mexico, but going there qualifies as a visit to another country, so off everyone goes. It's about as easy as international travel gets. All you need are some American dollars and a few Spanish phrases. A popular one is "¡Cerveza, por favor!"

On the other hand, you can stay in California and still savor a distinct Latin flavor. In fact, a lot of what's south of the border has already traveled north to California. The Latino influence is strongly felt in California, starting with meals. You can find great authentic Mexican food anywhere in California, and if you can't, well, you just haven't looked hard enough.

Population experts say that by 2040 Latinos will be a majority in California. Latino roots in the state are most evident in two neighborhoods, San Francisco's Mission District and East Los Angeles.

Playing off the tradition of Mexican muralists, San Francisco's Mission artists have transformed every blank wall into a vibrant canvas. For information and tours, contact the Precita Eyes Mural Arts Center (415–285–2287; www.precitaeyes.org). To feel transported to another land, visit the Mission during its annual Carnaval celebration (415–920–0125; www.carnavalsf.com).

The biggest Latino community in the United States is in East Los Angeles, birthplace of Olympic boxing champion Oscar de la Hoya and a driving force in the development of low riders in the 1950s. Still hugely popular, these slow-moving cars are known for their colorful, artistic paint jobs and ability to practically scrape the ground as they drive along.

Latino Culture:

Border culture is within easy reach for Californians.

you know you're in
california when...
...you've got the coolest job in the world

Your gorgeous co-workers all wear skimpy bathing suits. You make heroic rescues for a living, in between working on your tan. There's even time for a little interoffice romance.

You're dreaming, right? No, you're probably watching reruns of *Baywatch*, the television series about California lifeguards.

Then again, you could turn that fantasy into a reality and become a real California lifeguard, a popular career choice in a state with many miles of beaches. You can don stylish red swimsuits and look regal perched in your watchtower, scanning the sunny horizon for signs of trouble.

Lifeguards:

Most California lifeguards are hired for the summer only, but a few have made it a full-time career.

And yes, there is plenty of real danger out there, such as rip currents, pounding surf, and inexperienced swimmers who put themselves in harm's way. But hey, it's a still a day at the beach. Talk to someone who toils each day in a stuffy cubicle if you want a real sob story.

The modern era of lifesaving began in California with the arrival of Hawaiian George Freeth, hailed in California as the world's first official lifeguard. He was that, and more.

Freeth arrived in California in 1907, when many beach cities were promoting their seaside recreational facilities to a public untrained in basics such as swimming and staying afloat. He developed many of the techniques for modern lifesaving, including the torpedo buoy.

Freeth made one of the most dramatic rescues of his day, braving a storm to rescue several Japanese fishermen, a feat that earned him a Congressional gold medal.

Freeth introduced surfing, water polo, and the Australian crawl to Americans. Huge crowds flocked to the beach to watch Freeth surf, a skill that many Americans considered miraculous at the time. He was billed as the "man who can walk on water."

A bust of Freeth can be found at the Redondo Beach Pier, where Freeth began his California career as a lifeguard.

you know you're in
california when...
...a tree stands alone

California has the world's biggest and oldest trees. But the state's most famous tree isn't particularly big or old. It's just lonely.

Just off the rugged coast of Monterey Bay, on an unlikely perch of windswept rock, sits a single cypress tree. Appropriately named the Lone Cypress, the stunted tree has weathered bark supporting two moderate canopies of green set against the turbulent ocean.

The sight of this lone wooden warrior next to the roiling seas in a foggy mist makes for a dramatic view. After admiring the scene, most people pull out either a paintbrush or a camera to capture it. This is the world's most photographed tree and the most recognized growing thing in California.

The Lone Cypress is the most popular stop along 17-Mile Drive, a private loop road with lots of competition for scenic views. It includes peeks of the legendary Pebble Beach Golf Course, stunning coastal views, and a passage through the Del Monte forest.

Even if it had company, the Lone Cypress would still be unusual. It is a Monterey Cypress tree, a rare species found only in the Monterey Peninsula. Visitors have been coming to view the tree since the 1880s, when they arrived in horse-drawn carriages along a gravel road. Now they come mostly in cars and tour buses.

Lone Cypress:

California's most famous tree prefers to be alone.

The tree is probably around 250 years old, although no one is certain of its age. It has made a valiant stand here against the elements, battling storms and fierce winds and a root system secured in rock. The company that owns Pebble Beach supports the tree with a retaining wall. Visitors are also kept at a safe distance. This singular tree is treated as royalty. You can look, but don't touch.

you know you're in
california when...

...artists express themselves in really big ways

The drive along Interstate 10 gets very interesting around Cabazon. Here, the mundane scenery of gas stations and food stops is suddenly interrupted by the improbable sight of two giant cement dinosaurs.

You are not fatigued by the drive. They are really there, these objects of the creative vision of artist Claude Bell.

Bell toiled for 25 years to erect the mammoth beasts, a 65-foot-high *Tyrannosaurus rex* and a four-story-tall brontosaurus (a.k.a. *Apatosaurus*) that is 150 feet long (www.cabazondinosaurs.com/DinoHistory.html). For good measure Bell included a room in the belly of the brontosaurus that he envisioned as a restaurant but that is now used as a gift shop (706–251–4800).

Bell wasn't alone in his big thinking. Several California artists have worked on a larger-than-life scale to create truly monumental art.

Simon Rodia toiled by hand for thirty-three years to create tall, fanciful spires of encrusted tile, glass shards, rock, and seashells, known as the Watts Towers, at 1727 East 107th Street in Los Angeles.

Dentist Ken Fox erected towering cement sculptures around the Gold Rush town of Auburn, including several in the parking lot outside his dental office depicting Amazon women in action poses. His works weigh up to 100 tons each.

Antone Martin created several immense biblical figures now collected in a hillside setting in Yucca Valley known as Desert Christ Park (www.desertchristpark.org).

Sarah Winchester designed on a large scale, too, but she was compelled by strange advice. A mystic told her that to ward off evil from being heir to the Winchester rifle fortune, she would have to continuously remodel her house.

Workman toiled in San Jose for almost forty years, constructing a mishmash mansion that defies common sense. The Winchester House (408–247–2000; www.winchestermysteryhouse.com) has 160 rooms, 10,000 windows, 47 fireplaces, several stairways that lead nowhere, and doors that open up to walls.

Massive Monuments:

Some art and architecture in California is hard to miss.

you know you're in
california when...

...your burger is prepared in a time warp

While the McDonald's company points to a Des Plaines, Illinois restaurant opened by company founder Ray Kroc in 1955 as "where it all began," Californians know this is one big Filet-O-Fish tale.

The first McDonald's was opened in San Bernardino in 1940 by Richard and Maurice McDonald, who, for better or worse, pioneered the fast-food industry.

They came up with the Speedee Service System, which featured a jogging, pie-faced mascot wearing a big smile, bow tie, and tilted chef's hat. They offered a limited menu of burgers, fries, and shakes; did away with plates and silverware; and designed the distinctive neon yellow arch to lure customers from the road.

Customers liked the fast service and cheap prices (hamburgers were originally 15 cents), while other entrepreneurs were intrigued by the McDonald brothers' success. Among them was Kroc, who first approached the McDonalds as a salesman of milkshake makers but eventually bought the rights to the company from them for $2.7 million.

The original California McDonald's is gone, but the world's oldest surviving McDonald's is in Downey, California, opened in 1953 by the McDonald brothers as their fourth restaurant (10207 Lakewood Boulevard; 562–622–9248). It features the golden arches first drawn by Richard McDonald, as well as a 60-foot-high sign with the original Speedee mascot.

The yellow-and-white decor will take you back to the company's early days, as will its menu, with its focus on the basics that first propelled the McDonald brothers to fame: burgers, fries, and shakes. To enhance the time-skewed effect, workers don 1950s-style uniforms that feature paper hats and white shirts. There's also a gift shop and historical display.

It is a landmark to relish.

McDonald's:

Fast-food history is served up in paper wrappers in Downey, at the world's oldest McDonald's.

you know you're in
california when...
...seasonal visitors include those with blowholes

Despite their large size, whales are pretty hard to find in the ocean. Every year in California, thousands of people take on the challenge during a six-month period known as whale watch season.

Armed with powerful lenses and warm clothing, whale tourists depart in chartered boats up and down the California coast in a quest to spot migrating gray whales.

If successful, these benign whale hunts end with a wild clicking of cameras and lots of appreciative "Ooos!" and Ahhs!" The reward here is a glimpse of a flopping tail or a spout of water shooting into the air. The lucky ones are treated to a close-up view of a whale breaching out of the water, a rare and magnificent sight.

Hundreds of gray whales head south beginning in December to reach their mating grounds in Baja California, and most complete the round-trip journey back north by May.

California celebrates two other high-profile migrations: butterflies and birds.

Monarch butterflies from Canada prefer to winter in California. Pacific Grove residents keep a keen eye out for their arrival every fall. The town hosts a butterfly sanctuary of pine and eucalyptus trees and takes its guardianship of the butterflies seriously. A local law makes it a $1,000 fine to "molest a butterfly."

And don't even think of messing with a swallow's nest in San Juan Capistrano. It's against the law there. Each March hundreds of the birds return to nest in the town's old stone church, an event heralded by the ringing of church bells and lots of festivities. With a welcome like that, it's no wonder the swallows keep coming back.

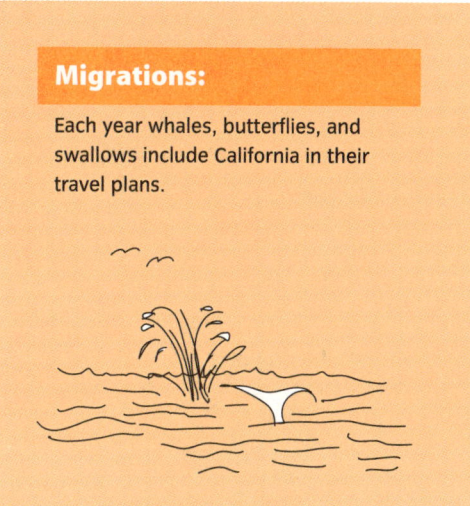

Migrations:

Each year whales, butterflies, and swallows include California in their travel plans.

you know you're in
california when...
...it's a small mall world

Let other regions of the country boast about having the biggest malls in the world. Southern Californians, especially those in the Los Angeles area, have a fondness for the scaled-down shopping zone known as the mini mall.

Some stores are just not ready for the big leagues of a regional mall. Unwilling to go it alone, they cluster in *U*-shaped one- or two-level structures that house about a dozen stores. There is parking, but never enough.

Mini malls have a no-frills design that is often criticized by those who prefer a little style in their urban shopping areas. But who cares about looks when there is so much useful commerce within easy access?

There is no rhyme or reason to which stores cluster together in a mini mall location. You'll find a donut shop next to a nail salon. A postal center adjacent to a dry cleaner. Other businesses that seem to favor mini malls are convenience stores, phone stores, video stores, and small drugstores.

Most mini malls include a curious ethnic restaurant or two. Southern Californians willing to ignore the bland decor of the mini mall setting have stepped into some of these restaurants and discovered hidden culinary gems. It is no shame in Southern California for an up-and-coming restaurant to be located in a mini mall.

Mini Malls:

Any intersection in Southern California is a good spot for a mini mall.

To be sure, Southern California has its share of big malls, too. In fact, California leads the nation in mall square footage.

Major malls in Southern California include The Beverly Connection, Del Amo Fashion Center, and the Gallerias of Sherman Oaks and Glendale. The swanky Grove in the Fairfax area of Los Angeles is proof that Southern Californians enjoy the big mall experience just like any other Americans with credit cards.

But when it comes to mall shopping, Southern Californians often go small.

you know you're in
california when...
...your room comes with an ice bucket

The nation's first motel debuted in San Luis Obispo in 1925 to some confusion.

California motorists were just getting used to the idea of car travel. In those early days of the automobile, the concept of a roadside lodging where you could drive up to your room seemed as foreign to them as, say, the car itself.

But workers at the Milestone Motel promoted the idea by handing out brochures to passing motorists chugging up a steep hill just outside the hotel. The motel's location halfway between Los Angeles and San Francisco offered a well-placed resting spot after a day of driving. Customers began stopping in.

Los Angeles architect Arthur Heineman and hotel developer James Vail had a grand scheme for a string of motels from San Diego to Seattle, each about a day's drive apart. They based their plan on Spanish missions, each built a day's horseback ride apart.

The Milestone was built in the Spanish Mission style, with a bell tower and red tile roof. It offered weary travelers a pretty comfy spot to take a break. Two-room bungalows included a kitchen, and the motel offered a pool, restaurant, and picnic area.

Heineman and Vail coined the term *motel* by contracting the words *motor* and *hotel*.

The Milestone Motel, which changed its name to the Motel Inn, was a little ahead of its time. The Depression hit before others could be built.

The modern American motel, with its basic roadside comforts of ice buckets, coffee machine, shower, bed, and phone, didn't come along until the 1950s. Now plenty of motel chains dot the area around the Motel Inn, which closed in the early 1990s.

There are plans to reopen this historic lodging. For now, visitors have to be satisfied with reading a plaque there that tells the story of the historic hotel, then getting back in their cars and finding a room somewhere else.

The Motel:
The idea for drive-up roadside lodging began in California.

you know you're in
california when...
...you get pumped up by the ocean breeze

If you reluctantly head to the gym each week and curse every sweat-drenched minute, you might as well blame California.

The roots of the modern American fitness boom can be traced to a stretch of sand just south of the Santa Monica Pier. It began in 1934 when a group of hyperactive, barrel-chested bodybuilders turned seaside excursions into something more strenuous than a typical day at the beach.

They began lifting weights and performing brawny gymnastic feats and stunts such as human towers to the delight of thousands of spectators. The locale earned the appropriate moniker of Muscle Beach.

This was the start of the American bodybuilding movement and fitness craze. The scene featured pioneers such as Jack LaLanne, Joe Weider, Vic Tanny, Steve "Hercules" Reeves, and many others, including college athletes, Hollywood stunt people, and even circus performers.

The site received funding from the Works Progress Administration. Widespread coverage of Muscle Beach, often featuring eye-popping photos of some of the area's muscled performers in bare-chested poses, helped the fitness craze muscle its way into the American mainstream.

Flab was out. Sculpted physiques were in. Santa Monica officials flexed their own power in 1959 by shutting down Muscle Beach after complaints surfaced about sexual misconduct there. Bodybuilders picked up their barbells and moved south to Venice.

Santa Monica revived its Muscle Beach in 2000 with a toned-down presence of gymnastic apparatus, including rings and parallel bars, as well as a historical marker denoting the original site.

The real lifting is done further south in an outdoor muscle pen north of the Venice Pier that features caged weight trainers grunting their way to more buffed bodies. They are often clothed in skimpy workout attire, the better to show off their progress. An appreciative crowd often gathers to watch.

Muscle Beach:
Acrobatic bodybuilders made a strong case for fitness on a Santa Monica beach beginning in 1934.

you know you're in
california when...
...there's a rush for black gold

Just as gold fever subsided in California, everyone became all hot and bothered about searching for another get-rich-quick substance: oil. It was the Gold Rush all over again, but this time with drillers, not miners.

Edward Doheny dug Southern California's first oil well in 1892, supposedly after he followed the trail of a cart that had tar on its wheels to an area near what is now Dodger Stadium. He drilled using a sharpened eucalyptus tree and found oil.

The gusher that triggered the state's oil rush erupted a few years later at Signal Hill near Long Beach. The Shell Oil Company drilled Alamitos #1, now known as the Discovery Well.

On June 23, 1921, the well sent a black geyser soaring more than 100 feet into the air. Soon after the gooey black drops hit the ground, thousands were rushing to Southern California to cash in.

Within two years there were more than 300 wells on Signal Hill. The area was so congested with spiked drill towers that it earned the nickname Porcupine Hill.

The Signal Hill oil field is legendary in the oil industry and recognized as the richest oil-producing area in the world. Discovery Well alone produced over 700,000 barrels of oil in its day. That helped make California the number-one oil-producing state in 1923,

Oil:

While California leads the nation in oil consumption, it's been good at producing it, too.

when it produced one-quarter of the world's total output.

Today California has slipped to fourth in oil production in the United States. Still, there are more than 46,000 working wells throughout California, and they are a common, if sometimes unexpected, sight.

The wells are usually clustered in small groups, looking like oversized metallic hammers probing the earth in rhythmic up-and-down motions, a part of the landscape.

you know you're in
california when...
...country music develops an edge

The sound emanating from Bakersfield in the 1950s was an electrified California challenge to country music's reigning center in Nashville.

Mainstream country music was frilly and full of strings in those days. Then Buck Owens arrived in Bakersfield, turned down the fiddles, and amped up his Fender Telecaster guitar. A new type of country music was born.

They called it the Bakersfield sound, and it was closely identified with stars like Owens and Merle Haggard, a Bakersfield native.

Owens was born in Texas, but Bakersfield was his adopted home and California's rebellious spirit was in his blood. He was an independent country music star who preferred the west to Nashville and Carnegie Hall to the Grand Ole Opry. He even played the White House.

Owens liked rock musicians, and they admired him. Creedence Clearwater Revival paid tribute to him in their song, *Lookin' Out My Back Door*.

Owens had a remarkable string of 21 number-one country music hits beginning in 1963. He also brought country music to the masses by co-starring in a hillbilly-style comedy-music show called *Hee Haw* that first aired in 1969.

Owens, Buck:

The country music scene got a lot more interesting after Buck Owens moved to California.

Despite his on-screen persona, Owens was no country bumpkin when it came to managing his career. He used money from his television career to build a media empire of radio and television stations that made him the richest man in Bakersfield.

During his later years he cut back on touring and built himself a concert hall in town, the Buck Owens Crystal Palace (2800 Buck Owens Boulevard; 661–328–7560), a combination steak house, museum, and musical venue.

Palace visitors can view his many stage suits and guitars, including his trademark red, white, and blue Fender, and other career memorabilia. Owens played there every Friday night with his band, the Buckaroos. He died on March 25, 2006, just hours after playing a final gig at the Palace.

you know you're in california when...
...you don't act your age

Television producer Riff Moskowitz went to Palm Springs to retire, or so he thought. It wasn't a bad idea, of course, since Palm Springs has long been known as a haven for retirees.

But perhaps there is something in the desert air that won't let people sit back and enjoy their golden years. Moskowitz, for example, ended up creating a theater show that has kept him busier than ever, *The Palm Springs Follies*.

The show has not only been a great success but it has inspired many seniors to rethink the notion of retirement. It has also reminded the world that Californians are an active bunch, no matter what their age.

Moskowitz launched the *Follies* in 1991 as a vaudeville-style dance and music review. Fair enough. It's just that Moskowitz enlisted only performers who were older than 55.

Many cast members began their careers in the vaudeville era and may have thought their performing days were long gone. Nope. Some dancers in the *Follies* are in their 80s. The show holds the distinction of having the oldest chorus line in the world.

You'd think this Social Security–eligible crew would at least be allowed to take it easy now and then, but that's not the case. They may be working harder in "retirement" than at any prior point in their lives.

Strong demand for tickets (760–327–0225; www.psfollies.com) has created a hectic performance schedule. Performers are on stage up to ten times a week for each three-hour show. For this bunch, the show must go on . . . and on and on.

Palm Springs Follies:

The performers in this show take the idea of "active retirement" to an extreme level.

you know you're in
california when...
...you dig holes by the scenic coast

There are golf courses, and then there is Pebble Beach. At least, that's how most golfers feel about this public course, which utilizes the windswept, craggy coastline of Monterey Bay as the setting for the most mystique-filled eighteen holes in the world.

The course opened in 1919 and has hosted several U.S. Open championships as well as a popular celebrity Pro-Am tournament.

Before they hang up their putters, most golfers dream about playing at least one round of golf at Pebble Beach. Perhaps that shows how most golfers are gluttons for punishment, because golf is hard enough without the extra challenges presented by the Pebble Beach Golf Links.

At Pebble Beach golfers must contend with biting winds, narrow fairways, postage stamp–sized greens, and the major distraction of breathtaking scenic coastal views that are the course's trademark. As golfers line up an important shot they may have their attention diverted by, say, migrating whales along the ocean or barking seals hanging out on the ocean rocks below. Several of the holes are laid out along the cliffs, turning the ocean into the world's largest water hazard.

It was Samuel Morse's vision that Pebble Beach would be a haven not only for seals and cypress trees but for golfers, too.

Morse, a distant cousin of the telegraph inventor, helped preserve the stunning coastal beauty in privately owned Pebble Beach and turn it into a public golfer's paradise.

Golfers who can't afford the fees at Pebble Beach (800–654–9300) sometimes settle for the Pacific Grove Municipal Golf Links (831–648–5777) a few miles away. The same golfer who planned Pebble Beach designed this course, and it offers its own scenic charms and golfing challenges.

Pebble Beach:

This California course is heaven on earth for golfers.

you know you're in
california when...
...your state flower is wild and unpredictable

In Western Antelope Valley they nervously scan the horizon each March, hoping to glimpse the first orange blooms that signal the arrival of poppy season.

No one is ever sure when the first California poppies will appear—or, when they do, how long they'll stick around, or how abundant they'll be.

Some years a psychedelic vista of swaying orange blooms blankets entire swaths of the desert grasslands and hillsides here. Other years the poppy barely shows at all, a major disappointment.

Everyone has a theory about what causes a bad flower year. Too cold in the fall. Not enough rain in the winter. Too windy. Not enough wind. It would help if they knew for sure, because a good flower season is a boon to the Lancaster area. When the poppy puts on a spectacular show, word gets out and thousands of people from around the world flock to the Antelope Valley California Poppy Reserve 15 miles west of Lancaster (wildflower hotline: 861–724–1180).

The park has 8 miles of trails through high-desert grounds that are prime spots for the California poppy. While other native wildflowers are also visible, as are assorted critters and the occasional rattlesnake, the poppy is the star.

The Poppy:

The California poppy season is mid-March through mid-May. Or maybe not.

You can start your journey at the park's Jane S. Pinheiro Interpretive Center, named for the woman who led the push to get this land turned into a poppy park in 1976. Pinheiro, who was also a poppy artist, was affectionately called the Poppy Lady.

The fickle poppy was selected as the state flower in 1903. Its distinctive orange-cupped blooms are a horticultural representation of the state's golden appeal.

California honors the shin-high flower with its own holiday on April 6, even if the flower has not yet appeared. More honors come at the annual California Poppy Festival (www.poppyfestival.com) held each April in Lancaster, an event with music, crafts, food, and, of course, a flower market.

you know you're in
california when...
...you elect to visit a presidential library

California's two presidential libraries have gone to great lengths to broaden their appeal beyond the scholarly set.

Promoters at the Richard Nixon Library and Birthplace in Yorba Linda, for example, describe it as offering a "dramatic roller coaster ride through half a century of California, U.S., and world history."

Meanwhile, the main attraction at the Ronald Reagan Library and Museum in Simi Valley isn't the treasure trove of historic documents there but the chance to climb aboard a real Air Force One.

The Nixon Library (18001 Yorba Linda Boulevard; 714–993–5075) opened in 1990 without any presidential papers, a seeming must for any presidential library. A 1974 law kept Nixon's archives in Washington, D.C. out of fear that Nixon would tamper with Watergate history. Plans to release the papers to the library were under way in 2006.

The Nixon library offers attractions such as a full-size replica of the White House's East Room, an elegant party space outfitted in chandeliers, silk drapery, and marble fireplaces. There's also a display of gowns worn by Pat Nixon during her reign as First Lady. You can tour the farmhouse built with a catalogue kit by Nixon's father in 1912 and where the future president was born a year later.

Presidential Libraries:

California's two presidential libraries are historical resources with theme-park panache.

There is loads of fun stuff, too, at the Reagan Library (40 Presidential Drive; 800–410–8354). It is a sprawling hillside site dedicated to the nation's 40th president and California's adopted son and former governor.

The Reagan Library does have lots of documents—50 million presidential papers, as well as 1.5 million photographs and hundreds of videos, books, and films. These artifacts trace Reagan's careers in sports broadcasting, films, and then politics.

But leave those documents for the researchers to salivate over. Visitors here instead thrill at the chance to climb aboard the Air Force One used as the flying White House from 1973 to 2001. You can also check out Reagan's 1984 parade limousine.

you know you're in california when...
...you create lots of outdoor scenes

Each spring thousands of people slather on sunscreen and flock to Hemet to bask in the outdoor glare and witness one of America's most unusual stage shows, California's official outdoor play, the melodrama *Ramona*.

"Unusual" in the sense that the production includes live horses, donkeys, and sheep. And the stage is actually a hillside and canyon where a few sets have been built. This piece of atypical theater was first staged in Hemet in 1923, making it what organizers say is the oldest outdoor play in the country.

Hemet's *Ramona* Pageant is based on Helen Hunt Jackson's 1884 novel that created a sensation, but not in the way she intended. Jackson wrote the novel to enlighten readers about the mistreatment of Southern California's native Indians and *ranchero* Mexicans at the hands of white settlers.

Readers instead fell in love with the story of Jackson's star-crossed lovers, Ramona and Alessandro. They also warmed to the Eden-like Southern California setting depicted by Jackson, which only attracted more Easterners to the region to muck things up for the natives, certainly not what Jackson had in mind.

Jackson's book fostered a *Ramona* industry of reenactments, tours, and three movies, and also set off a tourism and real estate boom in the area around Hemet, where the novel is set.

The Hemet play (800–645–4465) is the most enduring of the Ramona spinoffs. Hemet's stage version was written by Garnet Holme, who conceived of the idea of presenting the play in an outdoor natural amphitheater. While the audience initially sat on the ground, eventually the Ramona Bowl was built to provide better seating. Hats and other forms of sun protection are a must.

Ramona Pageant:

Helen Hunt Jackson's 1884 book, *Ramona*, was the first American novel set in Southern California.

you know you're in
california when...
...price tags have lots of zeros

Rodeo Drive (*always* pronounced "ro-DAY-o," never that other, cowboy way) in Beverly Hills is one of the world's most elite shopping districts, which is fine for those with a yen for status items and the budget to afford them.

For everyone else, Rodeo Drive is a gawker's paradise offering a window onto the world of retail extravagance.

Retailer Fred Hayman propelled Rodeo Drive to its high-end fame. He founded the Rodeo Drive Committee in the 1970s and turned the street's 3-block section in the heart of Beverly Hills into the world's premiere luxury shopping zone.

Hayman's Giorgio store, now closed, exemplified Rodeo's chichi atmosphere. The store contained an oak bar and billiards room that became a popular star hangout. Hayman chauffeured valued customers to his store in a yellow Rolls Royce.

Through the years Rodeo Drive stores cultivated a hard-earned reputation for being snobby, but the street's elite nature has been somewhat toned down. There are wider, more pedestrian-friendly streets for those just there to window-browse.

And more budget-minded stores have popped up along the street in recent years. The arrival of these stores has also created the odd arrangement of stores selling knockoffs located on the same Rodeo block as stores selling the real thing.

Still, high-end shops remain, including Bijan at 420 North Rodeo, which requires an appointment to get in and is probably the world's most expensive store. Other pricey stops include Tiffany, Prada, Hermès, and Louis Vuitton.

One priceless gem on Rodeo Drive is that rarity of a retail building designed by Frank Lloyd Wright, the Anderton Court at 322 North Rodeo Drive. Built in 1952, the three-story structure has been altered from Wright's original construction but still contains whimsical flourishes such as a projecting spire and zigzagging staircase. Enjoy the view—it's free.

Rodeo Drive:

Where luxury in California has its price, and it's a pretty steep one.

you know you're in
california when...
...zoo animals have more space than zoo visitors

At the San Diego Wild Animal Park, human visitors are apt to feel as if they are the ones locked in the zoo.

At the park hundreds of exotic beasts and birds roam free on a 1,800-acre expanse in Escondido. Meanwhile, people are confined to pathways or crammed onto trams that circle the outer edges of the wild landscape.

It's as if the animals are running the place—and, in a way, they are. Are you going to argue with an elephant for more space?

The pioneering animal park is an off-site breeding and conservation program for the San Diego Zoo, the city's forward-thinking 100-acre facility. The park (619–718–3000; www.sandiegozoo.org) houses animals such as giraffes, cheetahs, lions, and wildebeests, as well as many species of birds and plants.

The Wild Animal Park is designed to give its hoofed and winged residents an extensive home resembling their native habitat. The cageless philosophy behind the park was revolutionary when the facility opened in 1972, but it has since been emulated by other zoos around the country.

Visitors are invited to look around from safe vantage points. Closer views can be gained by participating in special sleepover programs that make it possible to experience the thrills of a safari without ever leaving California.

San Diego Wild Animal Park:

The residents of this pioneering zoo have staked out plenty of turf.

One such program is the popular Roar & Snore program. In this adventure, visitors camp out in an area overlooking the park's East Africa exhibit. While the snoring they hear may be that of a human neighbor in the next tent over, participants do meet animals, swap stories around a campfire, and get a feel of what it might be like to travel to an African wilderness.

The Roar & Snore programs are offered for families. Another option is a similar event for adults, where you can savor a wild savanna experience and enjoy a cocktail and hors d'oeuvres at the same time, quite the civilized way to go on a wild adventure.

you know you're in
california when...

...you walk the walk

It is common in San Francisco to see groups of pedestrians toting cameras and craning their necks while trailing a leader with a badge and a take-charge stride. These curious folks are using their feet to get a better view of the city.

San Francisco offers more walking tours than any other city in the country. Leading the pack is San Francisco City Guides 415–557–4266; www.sfcityguides.org), a group that began in 1978 by offering tours of City Hall.

The all-volunteer group has since considerably stepped up the pace. It now leads more than fifty different free walking tours that highlight the city's architecture, history, and lore. Topics range from Gold Coast architecture to one called "Bawdy and Naughty," an exploration of the city's Gold Rush–era red-light district.

Plenty of other tour groups have laced up their walking shoes, too, presenting a number of colorful ambling adventures.

Shirley Fong-Torres is the high-stepping chef and tour leader of Wok Wiz tours of Chinatown and North Beach (650–355–9157; www.wokwiz.com). The bonus here is that the tours include stops for food, most notably the popular "I Can't Believe I Ate My Way Through Chinatown." You'll eat

San Francisco Walking Tours:

The best way to experience this city is on foot.

dim sum and then walk some, and then perhaps more dim sum—you get the idea.

Other highlights include a vampire walking tour led by "vampire" Mina Harker (650–279–1840), a caffeine-infused excursion through North Beach called Java Walk (415–673–9255; www.javawalk.com), and a historical tour of San Francisco's gay community called Cruising the Castro (415–550–8110).

You can walk and hunt for ghosts (415–922–5590) or walk the old haunts of some of the city's famous literary figures (415–441–0140). Or how about walking and laughing with the crew from Foot, comedian-led walking tours (415–793–5378; www.foottours.com)?

you know you're in
california when...
...an ill wind gusts from the desert

From October through early spring, Southern Californians suffer the indignity of having a lot of hot air blown in their faces. Known as the Santa Anas, these blustery, searing currents make for bone-dry skin, bad hair days, and tense nerves.

The Santa Anas are also very efficient fire starters. The winds dry out vegetation, creating ready fuel for any spark. If a fire starts, the Santa Anas literally fan the flames, often leading to widespread burns that scorch thousands of acres.

Some people see an even more sinister side to the winds. Local lore says that the Santa Anas trigger earthquakes and drive people to commit violent crimes.

From a purely scientific standpoint, the term *Santa Ana winds* refers to strong warm currents that originate in high desert regions and then blow down upon lower elevations toward the coast. Sometimes these winds reach gale force (35 to 75 m.p.h., and that alone can cause great damage. Writer Raymond Chandler called them the Red Wind, saying they could "curl your hair and make your nerves jump and your skin itch."

The name *Santa Ana winds* probably comes from the Spanish name for them, the *Santana,* or "devil wind." Their hellish nature can't be overstated. Santa Ana conditions bring humidity levels down to about 10 percent, leaving everyone edgy, dry, and hot, not to mention furiously scratching at body parts.

The Santa Anas also confound normal California weather patterns. When they are blowing, normally cool coastal areas are often hotter than inland desert regions.

Hot winds blow all over the state. Near Santa Barbara they are called Sundowners, while further north in the San Francisco area they are known as Diablo winds.

By any name, it just means a lot of hot air coming your way.

Santa Ana Winds:

When Southern Californians feel the moisture sucked from their bodies, they know the Santa Anas are blowing.

you know you're in
california when...
...you're thrilled by history

The Santa Cruz Beach Boardwalk is an amusement park so lost in time that it takes visitors on a tilt-a-whirl journey into another dimension.

The park opened in 1907 and has updated its rides through the decades. The Fun House now features 3-D animation. The arcade offers laser tag and the latest in computer-animated games. Overall, though, the boardwalk has a timeless feeling that is just as exciting to experience as any of its thrill rides.

Santa Cruz's seaside amusement park (831–423–5590; www.beachboardwalk.com) once had rivals along the California coast, but they are all gone. A walk along Santa Cruz's boardwalk, munching on cotton candy and a dipped cone, is a sentimental journey through a living slice of California history. The entire boardwalk is a state historic landmark.

You can delight to the classics here, from bumper cars to water rides, or enjoy the simple pleasures of the park's two national landmark attractions, the Giant Dipper roller coaster and the Looff Carousel.

The Giant Dipper is a wooden beauty that takes riders on a two-minute, bone-jarring trip featuring rapid dips and soaring fan curves. Riders get the added bonus of a picture-perfect view of Monterey Bay from the 70-foot-high vantage point at the top of the coaster's first hill. Of course, you can't savor the moment, because suddenly you are shrieking as you head into the coaster's first white-knuckle plunge.

The carousel has seventy-three horses and two carriages and was hard-carved by Charles Looff in 1911. A vintage, 342-pipe organ provides the full-throttled carousel music, an essential component of any memorable merry-go-round.

Santa Cruz Beach Boardwalk:

More than 50 million riders have taken a wild spin on the amusement park's Giant Dipper wooden roller coaster, which opened in 1924.

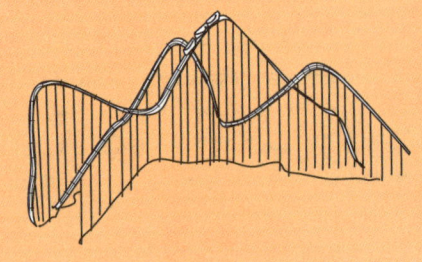

you know you're in
california when...
...where there's smoke, there's barbecue

There is no problem deciding what to serve for a special occasion in the Santa Maria area. A wedding? Barbecue. Birthday party? Barbecue. Elks Club meeting? Barbecue.

In these parts barbecue isn't so much a meal as a religion. Locals claim that their style of grilling meat is the purest form of barbecue and therefore the best.

Detractors may venture here armed with all kinds of sauces, muttering something about Kansas City this or Texas that. A bite of Santa Maria–style barbecue pretty much shuts them up. That is, until they want another bite.

Santa Maria barbecue dates to the area's cattle ranching days of the mid-nineteenth century, when cowboys were treated to barbecue feasts after working hard in the field. This ranch style of cooking is now an honored tradition practiced by just about everybody in town.

The recipe is simple enough. Meat is rolled in salt, pepper, and garlic salt and then placed on skewers and cooked over coals of native red oak. The rest of the meal features slow-cooked pinquito beans, green salad, buttered and toasted French bread, and salsa.

The only real decision is the cut of meat—either block sirloin or triangular bottom sirloin known as tri tip. A preference for one over the other can sometimes divide families. Yes, they take their barbecue seriously here.

Popular stops include the Far Western Tavern in Guadalupe (805–343–2211) and the Hitching Post in Casmalia (805–937–6151).

Of course, locals say that if you follow the aroma of red oak smoke anywhere in Santa Maria on a Friday or Saturday, prime grilling days, you are sure to find a barbecue.

Santa Maria–Style Barbecue:

This California town proudly proclaims itself the Barbecue Capital of the World.

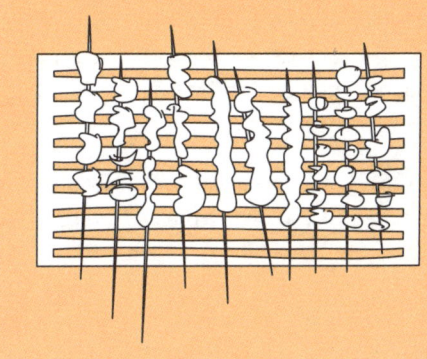

you know you're in
california when...
...you need a calendar to know the season

Californians get a little defensive when talk turns to the four seasons. You expect that, of course, considering that most people believe California doesn't have any.

A common lament from new arrivals in California goes: "Gee, California is nice, but I do miss the change in seasons." This complaint may be due to amnesia, since those longed-for seasonal changes include periods of bitter cold and stifling heat known as *winter* and *summer*.

The two primary seasons in California are *wet* and *dry*. Or, if you prefer, *hot* and *less hot*.

The wet season corresponds to what most people know as winter and spring, while the dry season occurs during summer and fall.

If the wet season isn't very wet, watch out! That could lead to a very dangerous fire season, which comes in summer and fall. If fire season is followed by wet weather, watch out again! That can only mean that mudslide season is on the way.

California weather can sneak up on people who aren't familiar with it. Visitors who pack T-shirts and shorts and head to San Francisco in July will be buying winter coats when they arrive. They'll be experiencing the chilly thrills of a cold summer in San Francisco, captured famously in the quote attributed to Mark Twain: "The coldest winter I ever spent was a summer in San Francisco." Funny, but true.

In a similar way, summer visitors to coastal Southern California might be bundling up if they arrive in time for June Gloom, a heavy marine layer that blocks out the sun and makes the start of summer feel like the onset of winter.

The arrival of Labor Day means saying goodbye to summer for most of the country, but in California September is usually when the summer's strongest heat wave is likely to strike.

Seasons:

California has seasonal changes, just not the ones most people are familiar with.

you know you're in
california when...

...nerds get their revenge

Geeks of the world owe their cool images and six-figure incomes to a string of industrial parks south of San Francisco known as Silicon Valley.

Geeks were once ridiculed as weirdos with pocket protectors and thick glasses. In a world enmeshed in high tech, geeks are now indispensable saviors. They still have pocket protectors, but they also boast an enhanced image as innovative free spirits who provide us with lots of new gizmos that make our lives better and more exciting.

The rise of high-tech companies clustered along Highway 101 fostered this image turnaround. Take Cupertino-based Apple Computer, which offered its first personal computer for sale in 1976. An early motto was: "Think Different," a slogan enhanced with an image of the world's coolest nerd, Albert Einstein.

The term *Silicon Valley* was coined in 1971, a reference to a basic material used to make computers, and the area's location in the Santa Clara Valley.

It all started in 1938 when Stanford grads William Hewlett and David Packard set up an electronics lab in a Palo Alto garage. That was the birthplace of Hewlett-Packard, and of Silicon Valley, too. The garage where it all began, a 12-by-18-foot wood-frame shed at 367 Addison Avenue, is now a state historic landmark.

Hundreds of high-tech companies now dot the horizon. In addition, two museums in the area offer visitors a glimpse inside this high-tech world of chips and electronic gadgets.

The Tech Museum of Innovation in San Jose (201 South Market Street; 408–294–8324; www.thetech.org) offers interactive exhibits showcasing the latest digital creations and how they affect our lives.

The Intel Museum in Santa Clara (2200 Mission College Boulevard; 408–765–0503; www.intel.com/museum/index.htm) presents lots of exhibits that trace the history of the company and explain how microprocessors work. For a fun time you can climb into a "bunny suit" worn by the chipmakers as you experience an "ultra-clean" room, the sanitized environment where chips are made. There's that coolness factor again

Silicon Valley:

The San Jose area has the world's largest concentration of technology companies, with close to 7,000 firms.

you know you're in
california when...
...you're surfing on the street

California's drought in the 1970s turned lawns brown and made it nearly impossible to get a glass of water at a restaurant. And this severe water shortage also helped revolutionize the sport of skateboarding.

Skateboarding was first introduced in the 1950s by California surfers and hung around for a few years before dying out. Skateboarding was viewed as a fun way for bored surfers to pass the time until they could climb back on their boards and surf again.

Then in the 1970s a group of kids in Santa Monica injected the edgy attitude and aggressive skating styles that have made the sport so popular today. The introduction of urethane wheels and better board designs helped fuel skateboarding's transformation. So did the drought.

The Santa Monica skaters discovered that some of the best places to practice their new moves were empty swimming pools drained because of the water shortage. Tilted asphalt walls at playgrounds and parking lots were good training grounds, too.

The Santa Monica skaters were known as the Z-Boys, or the Zephyr skate team, and they called their seaside Santa Monica turf "Dogtown." Their history is detailed in the documentary *Dogtown and Z-Boys*.

The film recalls how the Zephyr team competed at the 1975 Del Mar Nationals and stunned the crowd with their aggressive, low-slung style of boarding, standing out like "a hockey team at a figure skating show."

That swagger and outsider coolness are what define modern skateboarding and have helped popularize the sport with youngsters. In fact, you might as well say that the whole era of extreme sports can be traced to Santa Monica's Zephyr skate team.

Skateboarding was further moved along by the sport's most famous athlete, Tony Hawk, a San Diego native who dominated competitions in the 1980s and 1990s.

Skateboarding:
The surfing sport on wheels got its style and attitude in California.

you know you're in
california when...
...the air is thick

Not that it is anything to brag about, but Los Angeles is a national leader when it comes to air pollution. While smog limits visibility and makes normal breathing a challenge, a silver lining to this brown cloud is that dirty skies produce extraordinary sunsets, probably the finest in the world.

But first, the bad news. The Los Angeles area was plagued by smog even before there were cars. European explorers commented on smoky conditions in the Los Angeles basin in the sixteenth century. The bowl-like basin and heavy overhead inversion layer are perfect for trapping bad gas.

Industrial fumes in 1903 fouled the air so badly that residents thought there was an eclipse of the sun. The infamous "gas attack" on July 26, 1943, when visibility was reduced to 3 blocks in downtown Los Angeles, convinced civic leaders that something had to be done to clear the air.

Since then, there have been myriad measures to limit not only noxious fumes from cars but any potential smog culprit, including lawn mowers, outdoor grills, and even nail polish. More desperate folks, in between wheezing and rubbing their eyes, have suggested drastic measures such as using cannons to shoot holes in the inversion layer to allow bad air to escape.

Smog:
An unpleasant fact of Los Angeles life that makes for memorable sunsets.

Things are better today, but far from clear. Living in Los Angeles means watching weather reports to see what the smog forecast will be. It can range anywhere from good to hazardous, the latter meaning "stay indoors and try not to breathe."

Coughing Angelinos have taken solace in the one upside to smog: the area's famed sunsets. On heavy smog days, sunsets can be otherworldly and brilliant—flashing vibrant purples, pinks, and even greens and blues. It is something to appreciate, if you can open your eyes long enough to view it.

you know you're in
california when...
...dinner really is a smorgasbord

A town with windmills, restaurants that serve authentic Danish food, and a museum that pays tribute to Hans Christian Andersen; this could only be one place in the world—Solvang, California.

Yes, so much Danish culture in California's Santa Ynez Valley comes as a surprise to some people. But there's a fairy-tale story behind this seemingly out-of-place town, one that Andersen would surely appreciate.

A group of Danish immigrants settled the town in 1911, heading west after tiring of the bitter cold of America's Midwest. They must have thought they'd come upon a sunny slice of heaven when they arrived in California, because they named the town *Solvang*, which means "sunny field" in Danish.

Today Solvang looks a bit kitschy from afar, but there's a genuine dedication to all things Danish here with cultural offerings, special events, and authentic Danish restaurants and bakeries.

The town hosts an annual Danish Days celebration each September. The event dates back to 1936, when the Danish king and queen dropped by to help the town celebrate its twenty-fifth anniversary.

The Elverhøj Museum (1624 Elverhoy Way; 805–686–1211; www.elverhoj.org), pronounced "EL-ver-hoy," offers exhibits that

Solvang:
You can tilt at windmills and lap up Danish culture in this California town.

explore Danish culture and the town's history. Upstairs at the Book Loft (1680 Mission Drive; 805–688–2052) is a museum dedicated to Hans Christian Andersen, the fairy-tale master. It displays letters, first-edition works, and artwork.

You can taste Danish culture at the town's eateries. Everything from Danish butter cookies to smorgasbord is available here, as well as something known as *aebleskiver*, which locals describe as pancakes in the shape of little balls. They are often covered with powdered sugar and jam for one sweet bite of Danish culture.

you know you're in
california when...

...you prefer your bread on the tangy side

When you bite into a slice of San Francisco sourdough bread, the bread bites back.

The bread's distinctive sour taste, coupled with its crunchy golden crust and soft chewy center, has been a winning combination since the city's Gold Rush days. The bread was so popular with gold miners that they were nicknamed "Sourdoughs." Good thing for them they didn't favor pumpernickel.

The key ingredient to sourdough's sweet success is a wild yeast found only in San Francisco. No one is quite sure why it grows only here, but it probably has something to do with the city's perpetual fog.

French baker Isidore Boudin first harvested the magical sourdough yeast in 1849 and used it to make the seminal loaf. Amazingly, Boudin's original starter dough has been continuously replenished and preserved as "mother dough." The venerable San Francisco bakery (800–992–1855; www.boudinbakery.com) now churns out more than 10,000 fresh loaves daily, and each one contains a portion of Boudin's original yeast mixture.

The mother dough was almost toast during San Francisco's 1906 earthquake, but Louise Boudin rescued it and stashed it safely away in a bucket. A few generations later, the mother dough got star treatment when it was ceremoniously carted in a vintage wagon to Boudin's new flagship store at 160 Jefferson Street at Fisherman's Wharf.

The site includes a demonstration kitchen that features a 300-foot-long observation window visible from the street. Visitors can peer in as bakers shape loaves by hand.

You can also chew on some San Francisco history here with a stop at Boudin's Sourdough Museum. This dough-themed exhibit space features vintage photos and artifacts that highlight the close relationship between sourdough bread and San Francisco's development from the Gold Rush to the present.

Sourdough Bread:

No mere bookend for a sandwich, sourdough bread demands to be tasted on its own terms.

you know you're in california when...
...you're on a mission

Before it ultimately became hitched to the United States, California had several other suitors. And why not? With coastal access and lots of fertile ground and natural resources, pre-California was one desirable chunk of real estate.

While countries making overtures included Great Britain and Russia, the foreign power making the strongest pitch was Spain. From its base in Mexico, Spain launched an expansion effort into California in the early eighteenth century that called for the building of religious outposts, or *missions*, spaced a day's horseback ride apart.

The first Spanish mission, Mission San Diego de Alcala, was built in San Diego in 1769. The last, as far north as Sonoma, was called San Francisco Solano; it was completed in 1823. The 600-mile route connecting California's twenty-one missions was called El Camino Real. Today Highway 101 follows that route.

The missions' main mission, so to speak, was the conversion of native Indians to Christianity. A secondary purpose was to scare off other international powers from moving into California. Each outpost was a way of saying: "Hands off! She's mine."

The settlements contained buildings of simple adobe design and each included a church and living quarters. Missions were designed to be self-sufficient, so they included major agricultural efforts, including the planting of California's first vineyards. Wine was a popular table drink at missions, easing the burdens of outpost living.

When Mexico gained independence from Spain, the missions were eventually turned over to private owners in the 1830s. After the United States seized control of California in 1848, most of the missions fell into disrepair.

The status of each mission can be tracked by logging on to www.missionsofcalifornia.org. This helpful site offers a brief history of each mission and directions for visiting.

California's remaining missions are all state landmarks. A visit offers a glimpse back in time when the state was up for grabs.

Spanish Missions:

If the mission plan had worked, California today would be a part of New Spain.

you know you're in
california when...
...you're waving a checkered flag

The first go-kart in the world wasn't much to brag about. It had a lawn mower engine and a top speed of 35 miles per hour. No matter. This mini car with no suspension that carried its driver inches off the ground was a thrill to race.

Art Ingels built the premiere go-kart in Southern California in 1956. Soon after, every other go-kart in the world—all twelve of them—was noisily revving its engine in the parking lot of the Rose Bowl in Pasadena for the start of the first go-kart race in history. The karts roared around a makeshift course and a new motor sport was born.

The first go-kart maker opened in Monrovia, selling mail-order kits for $129. Today go-karts are raced by millions of people across the country, and they remain hugely popular in California, which has several tracks for professional and amateur thrill-seekers.

Go-karts are used as training vehicles for drivers looking to move into Indy car racing, or just as a way to get your kicks. The Jim Hall Kart Racing School (805–654–1329; www.jhrkarting.com) is the country's longest-running kart-training facility. It offers a scenic beachside course, as if you had a moment to check out the scenery. Forget it. Keep your eyes on the racecourse as you peel around the track at speeds of up to 100 mph.

Speed Racing:
Californians have come up with creative ways to race on four wheels.

Even before go-karts came along, California hot rods were racing along dry lake beds and other open areas. This lead to the development of the sport of drag racing in the 1930s. The first official drag race was held at an air base in Goleta in the 1940s, introducing another popular American motor sport with California roots.

Yet another big racing event created in California is off-road competitions. These events began in the 1960s, when drivers decided to forgo a track altogether and head into the rugged wilderness to see who was fastest to the finish.

you know you're in
california when...
...fiction and reality intersect

They tell writers to write what they know, and John Steinbeck certainly banked on that advice throughout a distinguished career.

Steinbeck won a Nobel Prize for literature in 1962. Not bad for a farm boy from rural Salinas. His parents hoped he would one day become a doctor, but millions of readers are glad he ended up writing more complex prose than prescriptions.

Instead of healing bodies, he focused on healing souls by writing morality tales drawn from his own experiences as a longtime Californian. An early novella, "The Red Pony," was inspired by a horse he had in childhood. His reporting for a San Francisco newspaper on the migration of Dust Bowl Oklahomans heading to California led to his widely acclaimed work, *The Grapes of Wrath*.

His breakthrough book in 1935, *Tortilla Flat*, developed from characters he knew around Salinas, as did *Of Mice and Men* and *East of Eden*. Salinas honors him with an exhibit space called the National Steinbeck Center, at 1 Main Street (831–796–3833). Exhibits trace the intersection of fiction and reality in Steinbeck's world.

The colorful characters and atmosphere contained in his *Cannery Row* stories, published in 1945, might have seemed a clever

Steinbeck, John:

The people, politics, and social themes of California fueled the imagination of one of America's greatest writers.

invention to readers, but they were more like nonfiction for residents of the real Cannery Row in Monterey, where Steinbeck spent a lot of time. The vivid portrait of "Doc" was based on Steinbeck's longtime friend, biologist Ed Ricketts, who maintained a laboratory in Monterey. Other people and locations were part of the scene of Monterey's once-booming sardine industry.

While commercialization has covered over much of the actual remnants of Steinbeck country, some evidence remains, including Ricketts's lab, a weather-beaten shack at 800 Cannery Row.

you know you're in
california when...
...everything is just swell

When the surf's up in California, so is the absentee rate at schools and offices. Dude, work will always be there. Great waves might not.

For many Californians, surfing isn't just a sport but a way of life. California surfing culture has spawned its own language and attire and also touched off regional disputes.

There are surfing hot spots up and down the California coast, where you are apt to see dozens of boarders in wet suits bobbing away, waiting for the next great wave to ride ashore.

Surfing was introduced to California in the early 1900s by Hawaiians who came to the mainland to demonstrate what was a long tradition in Polynesian culture. The sport exploded here in the 1950s and 1960s with the advent of commercially produced surfboards and greater publicity, including network broadcasts of surfing championships.

The laid-back persona of the California surfer doesn't always hold true. There are frequent reports of locals along the coast fiercely guarding their coveted surfing spots from any intrusion. Not-so-subtle warnings may include riding outsiders off their boards or slashing their car tires.

Civic leaders too have engaged in gnarly battles over surfing rights. Leaders of Huntington Beach and Santa Cruz have tussled over which California town can be called Surf City, USA. Each side says the other is all wet.

Several cities host competing surfing museums, with some vying to be designated the official surfing museum of the state. Exhibit spaces in Huntington Beach, Oceanside, Santa Cruz, Santa Barbara, and San Clemente all trace the history of surfing in California with photos and artifacts.

Beach towns also sell loads of surfing apparel, so you can dress like a surfer even if you don't know a thing about hanging ten.

Surfing:
The call of the surf is heeded by many board-carrying Californians.

you know you're in
california when...

...there are many escapes from reality

Main Street, Disneyland is the most visited street in California. That's what happens when you throw a parade every day and keep the sidewalks spotless.

There's more, of course—as in fun rides, strolling Disney characters, and an overall cheerful atmosphere. Above all, Walt Disney wanted his kingdom to be a happy one.

Disneyland (714–781–4565; www.disneyland.com) opened in 1955 and launched the age of the modern American theme park, one very much embraced in California.

With all the theme parks in California, there is enough fantasy land to make another state, and a pretty amusing one at that. You need walk only a few yards from Disneyland to run smack into another theme park, Disney's California Adventure, where you can tour an amusement park version of the state.

A short car ride transports you to yet another fantasy world: this one, the venerable Knott's Berry Farm (714–220–5200; www.knotts.com) in Buena Park. The twist here is that Knott's began as an Old West attraction designed as a diversion for diners waiting to be seated at a popular chicken restaurant. Now the chicken can wait until after the thrill rides.

The theme at Legoland (760–918–5346; www.lego.com) in Carlsbad is built around colorful plastic building blocks. Visitors stroll around 128 acres filled with stuff made out of Legos, even the rides. A highlight is Miniland, miniature versions of American landmarks crafted from Lego pieces.

Universal Studios Hollywood (800–864–8372) began as a tram tour of its studio lot and has grown into a major park that offers rides and attractions built around a moviemaking theme. It also offers its own unreal Main Street in the form of Universal CityWalk, a block of restaurants, shops, and nightclubs.

You can drop by SeaWorld (619–226–3901; www.seaworld.com) in San Diego and Six Flags Marine World (707–643–6722; www.sixflags.com/parks/marineworld) in Vallejo for parks with a more nautical theme. Both sites have superstar killer whales and lots of frisky dolphins.

Theme Parks:

California is a fantasy world for amusement park visitors.

you know you're in
california when...
...thousands of flowers go floating by

In 1890 members of a Pasadena hunting club were so thrilled about California's warm winter weather that they decided to organize a parade. That kind of exuberance is common among new arrivals from colder climates to the east, as these people were. They tend to become giddy about being outside in January without multiple layers of clothing.

The first Pasadena parades were processions of horse-drawn carriages covered in flowers, followed by exotic contests that included races between camels and elephants. There's that giddy part again.

These are the roots of what is now one of the most watched events in the world, the Tournament of Roses Parade. The objective today is not to boast about California's weather but to see who can create the most fascinating motorized floats completely covered in flowers and seeds.

Each year professional designers and thousands of volunteers vie to outdo each another with elaborately planned and colorfully animated floats, often with spectacular results. Regardless of who the winner is, there's little time to savor the moment. The flowers from one parade haven't even dried before planning begins for next year.

The parade, held on New Year's Day or a day later if January 1 falls on a Sunday, is watched by thousands of people who line the 5½-mile route along Orange Grove and Colorado Boulevards. Millions more watch on television.

Many people opt for a closer look by buying tickets to view the floats either before the parade or after it. (Contact the parade office at 626–449–4100.) The parade is always followed by the annual Rose Bowl game, first held in 1902 as the first post-season college football contest.

A more recent Pasadena tradition is the Rose Parade's thornier cousin, the annual Doo Dah parade (http://www.pasadenadoo dahparade.info), held on a Sunday around Thanksgiving. This parade, begun in 1978, is an irreverent procession of zany costumes and goofy marching bands meant as a spoof of the city's traditional event.

Tournament of Roses Parade:

Pasadena's annual event of petal power is one of America's favorite parades.

you know you're in
california when...
...you worship a grocery store

Food shopping at California's legendary grocery chain Trader Joe's is hardly a mundane chore. It's more like attending a festive event where everyone just happens to have a shopping cart.

It's not a burdensome duty but a thrilling quest to discover new and exciting forms of nourishment and caloric indulgence.

Cedar plank walls, hand-painted signs, and the Polynesian garb of its employees give the stores a quaint feel. The many one-of-a-kind items sold here foster customer loyalty verging at times on cult exuberance.

Shelves are crammed with must-have products that customers didn't know they must have until Trader Joe's began selling them, such as peanut butter–stuffed pretzels, teriyaki turkey jerky, and wild blueberry juice.

Mainstay items include whole-bean coffees, nuts, trail mixes, juices, cheeses, wines, crunchy snacks, and pre-prepared entrees and appetizers. Each item sold in the store must pass muster with the chain's own tasting panel of foodies, who scrutinize every morsel before it's cleared for sale. Trader Joe's (www.traderjoes.com) offers more than 2,000 unique items at discounted prices produced under its own label, allowing customers to eat like a gourmet without spending like one.

Trader Joe's:

Heading to "TJ's" several times a week is common behavior in California.

The original "Trader Joe" was Joe Coulombe, who launched the convenience store chain (yes, it started out as a convenience store) in the Los Angeles area in 1958. The chain opened its first store outside the state in 1993 and has continued to expand across America, one Thai Lime & Chili Peanut at a time.

The chain's expanding reach isn't long enough for some stranded fans, who travel great distances to stock up on Trader Joe's specialty items as if they were preparing for an extended siege. It's an indulgence that any longtime Trader Joe's shopper appreciates.

you know you're in
california when...
...a day in the park means more than a picnic

San Diego's Balboa Park and San Francisco's Golden Gate Park have lots of grass and trees and pretty flowers. And there are plenty of sports fields and lush walkways. That much you expect from any place with the word *park* in it.

But these unique destinations are really more playgrounds for the mind. They each feature dozens of cultural centers designed to exercise your brain instead of your body.

You could still drop by and spread a blanket, nibble on some cheese, and then grab a nap. But that idea seems so European. In California a park outing is so much more vigorous and challenging.

Why lounge when you could visit one of fifteen museums contained in Balboa Park? They range from the San Diego Hall of Champions Sports Museum (619–234–2544; www.sdhoc.com) to the Museum of Man (619–239–2001; www.museumofman.org).

You can brush up on your Shakespeare at the park's Old Globe theater (619–234–5623; www.theoldglobe.org) or check out more than 4,000 rare and endangered animals at the park's San Diego Zoo. Giant pandas are popular residents.

Balboa Park also features one of the world's largest outdoor pipe organs at the Spreckels Organ Pavilion (619–702–8138; www.sosorgan.com). The organ's largest pipe is 32 feet long, while the smallest is the length of a pencil. There are free afternoon concerts here every Sunday.

There's no point in just resting at Golden Gate Park, either. A highlight is the California Academy of Sciences (415–321–8000; www.calacademy.org), scheduled to open new park digs in 2008. An old standby is the Conservatory of Flowers (415–666–7001; www.conservatoryofflowers.org), at the park since 1879, making it the oldest glass-and-wood Victorian greenhouse in the United States.

At the western end of the park, don't miss the rare sight of an urban herd of bison. There has been a small group of these woolly, broad-shouldered beasts here since 1892.

Urban Parks:

Balboa Park and Golden Gate Park have a lot going on.

- SPRECKELS ORGAN
- SAN DIEGO ZOO
- OLD GLOBE THEATER
- MUSEUM of MAN

you know you're in
california when...
... you let strangers in red vests park your car

Parking a car in Los Angeles is not like parking a car anywhere else. In other parts of the country, you actually look for a spot to park your car.

In Los Angeles you don't search for a parking space but hunt for a sign. The sign will say VALET PARKING. A smiling person in a red vest will greet you, open your car door, and hand you a white ticket stub.

All you do is exit the car, happily hand over the keys, and head to your destination with a bounce in your step, as if you hadn't even driven there at all.

Los Angeles is probably the valet parking capital of the world. Here you valet park everywhere, at dry cleaners and hospitals, apartment buildings and the gym. Show up at a birthday party for a two-year-old and a valet will be there to park your car. Just grab your gift and go.

There is even valet parking in places where there is plenty of parking available, such as a parking lot. This seems silly, but valet parking is mostly about arriving in style. You want to appear as if you couldn't be bothered by something as ordinary as parking.

There are times when you don't valet your car in Los Angeles. That's when you are driving a car that doesn't reflect well on

Valet Parking:

The only people who park cars regularly in Los Angeles are valets.

your social standing, an older model with too much visible wear and tear.

That's why many people in Los Angeles overextend their credit in order to drive something fancy. Then you can valet without shame and earn the ultimate tribute—your car won't be parked at all, but left right there next to the valet station for all to admire. When you emerge, people will notice who picks up the keys and drives away.

you know you're in
california when...
...Italian culture doesn't translate well

Venice, California was supposed to be a lot like Venice, Italy. At least, that's how its founder, Abbot Kinney, envisioned it back in the early 1900s.

Kinney planned an enlightened enclave of canals, Venetian architecture, and high-minded cultural offerings. Sixteen miles of canals were dug on former marshland and Kinney's dream—or his folly, as some snickered—opened in 1904.

It was a magical planned community with imported gondolas and its own miniature rail system. Kinney added Coney Island flourishes such as an amusement pier, and for a while his dream took hold. But then the canals started to stink and Kinney discovered that American crowds weren't so interested in high-minded entertainment. They seemed to prefer camel races.

Fascination with cars made the canals less appealing, and soon most of them were filled in and then paved over to make roads. Venice was eventually annexed by the city of Los Angeles in 1925, its brief fling with European culture officially over.

In the end, Venice became a unique California town, a seaside haven for counterculture expression that makes it the most edgy and eclectic coastal community in the state, if not the country.

Jazz cats and beatniks hung out there in the 1950s, followed by hippies a decade later. The Doors' Jim Morrison had a psychedelic turn there, along with others who gave Venice an artistic bohemian component.

Today the Venice boardwalk is a carnival of incense hawkers, bikini-clad inline skaters, New Age healers, T-shirt sellers, street performers, and assorted free spirits.

Remnants of Kinney's original vision remain in the area's architecture of enclosed colonnades, and in the few remaining canals south of Venice Boulevard, which underwent a major restoration in the 1990s.

But now the face of Venice is a three-story-tall moving statue on Main Street that features the head of a male clown on a female ballerina's body. Landmarks like these make Venice truly its own place.

Venice:

Venice, California shares its name with Venice, Italy, but has forged its own special identity.

you know you're in
california when...
...homes have loads of curb appeal

If you want to know what life was like in late nineteenth-century California, you could read about it in books. Or you could just drop by Ferndale and see for yourself.

This seemingly lost-in-time village in Humboldt County was settled in 1850. It feels like nothing has changed since, except maybe a fresh coat of paint here or there.

The lost-in-time ambience has a lot to do with the town's many well-preserved Victorian-era buildings, a showy architectural style that was popular in California in the late 1800s as the state's population exploded.

There's nothing laid-back about Victorian architecture, which calls attention to itself with features such as frilly ornamentation, splashy colors, stained glass, and gabled roofs. The style suited Ferndale residents in the town's early days, when many prospered as dairy farmers. The Victorian homes they built were called "butterfat palaces."

Californians rediscovered a passion for their Victorians in the 1960s. In Ferndale, for instance, many of the town's Victorian structures were threatened by new development until community members organized a "paint-in" in 1962 to spruce them up. The strategy worked. The Victorians looked too pretty to smash, so they were preserved.

Today Ferndale is California's best-preserved Victorian village. In fact, the whole town is a state historic landmark. One of Ferndale's most photographed buildings is the Gingerbread Mansion (707–786–4000), now an inn.

There are well-preserved Victorian buildings throughout California. The greatest collection is in San Francisco, although many of its Victorians were destroyed in the 1906 fire and earthquake.

Still, thousands remain. Probably the most famous are a row of "painted ladies" in Alamo Square, set against the more modern city skyline. This is one of the most photographed residential blocks in the world.

Victorian Architecture:
The Victorian era is very much alive in many California neighborhoods.

you know you're in
california when...
...you really want to blow your top

The 1997 disaster flick, *Volcano*, in which a lava eruption slimes modern-day Los Angeles, seems like pure popcorn entertainment, except that the story line is not far from reality.

California has several active volcanoes, including one that erupted in 1915, which geologically speaking is like only a second or two ago. That was Lassen Peak, a volcano in Shasta County that scientists considered dormant, until it woke up in a big way.

Lassen Peak began rumbling in 1914 and a year later had a major explosion that sent a mushroom cloud of noxious gas more than 7 miles into the air, causing ash to fall 200 miles away. It continued to stir until 1921 and then called it quits. For now.

Californians don't walk around with helmets on while casting wary glances at the sky, nervously awaiting the next explosion.

Almost all of California's volcanoes expended their destructive energy centuries ago. So it's relatively safe today to explore in the shadow of the state's slumbering volcanoes.

If you really believe Lassen Peak is quiet for good, you can visit Lassen Peak National Park (530–595–4444; www.nps.gov.lavo). The park includes Mount Lassen, the world's largest lava dome, and eerie landscapes created by previous eruptions.

Volcanoes:
The state's many volcanoes have shaped California's landscape, and some aren't quite finished with their work.

These sites have appropriate names, such as the Devastated Area and Chaos Jumbles.

Another volcanic wonderland is Lava Beds National Monument in Tulelake (530–667–2282; www.nps.gov/labe). It features more than 500 volcanic caves formed long ago when lava crusted over to form large tubes of volcanic rock.

Mammoth Mountain is a volcanic dome that is considered potentially active today. Nearby is the peculiar Devils Postpile National Monument (760–934–2289), whose precisely crafted rows of rock columns were formed naturally when the structure served as a dam for cooling lava from a volcano upstream. A Hollywood set designer couldn't have done a better job.

you know you're in
california when...
...you go to war over water

Behind the simple gesture of turning on a faucet in California is a complex delivery process of engineering marvels and political intrigue.

Who knew water could be so complicated? The simple fact is that California's development into an economic and agricultural powerhouse would be impossible without its massive and controversial water distribution system.

At the heart of the process is the California Aqueduct, a 444-mile concrete channel that sends northern water gushing to farmlands in the Central Valley and heavily populated regions in the state's southern section.

Needless to say, folks to the north aren't always pleased with this arrangement because, well, technically it's really their water. And fish and other wildlife in depleted northern waterways aren't too happy about the deal, either.

Yet the water keeps flowing southward, powered by an elaborate system of pumps and siphons and including a gravity-defying climb over the Tehachapi Mountains. Political conflict aside, the aqueduct is truly an amazing engineering feat.

So much water moves through the aqueduct that stations along the way generate loads of hydroelectric power for the state.

Water Wars:

Water fights break out all the time in California during high-stakes battles for a precious resource.

The aqueduct is also the state's longest river. You can fish in parts of it or even ride a bike alongside it. A long, open portion of the aqueduct is visible from Interstate 5, a major north-south artery, and this view helps break the monotony of an often-dull drive.

Political conflict and water are also enmeshed in Los Angeles history, a backstory plotted in the movie *Chinatown*. The city's first aqueduct, completed in 1913, drained the lake in Owens Valley and led to a short-lived revolt by residents there who felt cheated out of their water rights.

Today thirsty Los Angeles sucks up water from the California Aqueduct, the Colorado River, the Owens Valley, and Mono Basin. Meanwhile, water wars continue in the state, pitting the north against the south and farmers against urban dwellers.

you know you're in
california when...
...you're jumping out of your stadium seat

The atmosphere was already tense at the Oakland Coliseum on October 15, 1981. The Oakland A's were competing in a heated baseball playoff game against the New York Yankees.

More drama was added that day when A's cheerleader Krazy George Henderson banged his drum and directed the crowd to do something new and peculiar. He gestured wildly for them to stand up and sit down in a rhythmic pattern rippling around the stadium.

Like awkward dancers learning a new move, the crowd stumbled. Henderson's ambitious plan was, after all, visionary thinking for a cheerleader. Fortunately, Henderson came armed with a plan to make it work.

He directed a chorus of boos at the section where the movement had died, shaming them to participate. Finally everyone joined in, with each sections rising and falling in a marvelous, swelling motion that undulated around the stadium

The Wave was born.

Yes, the ultimate display of crowd conformity, the Wave, was invented in independent-minded California. Henderson, a professional cheerleader, first got the idea as a student cheerleader at San Jose State University. He waited for the Oakland A's playoff game to launch its professional debut.

"It took about four tries to get it going," Henderson says of the initial efforts that day. "I knew what I wanted, but no one had ever seen it before. The first time it went about five sections and then it died."

When it finally worked, Henderson said, "the place just went nuts."

The Wave still thrills audiences today, showing that this California cheer has staying power.

The Wave:

The world's first successful stadium wave swelled in California.

you know you're in
california when...
...nature isn't very natural

With so many unconventional people in California, it is not surprising that the state's natural wonders tend toward the eccentric as well. Nowhere is this more evident than in the state's desert regions.

Take an area of Death Valley National Park known as the Racetrack. It's a dry, oval-shaped lake bed surrounded by mountains. Rocks scattered along the lake bed's clay surface appear to stage mysterious dance routines when no one is looking. Trailing these rocks are grooved tracks in fanciful patterns, as if the rocks had somehow slid along the surface in a desert ballet. Scientists are baffled as to how the rocks move.

Another closet entertainer is the Kelso Dunes in the Mojave Natural Preserve, also known as the Singing Sands. These massive dunes are impressive enough as a visual backdrop, soaring 600 feet into the air. But they also sing when you walk on them, or at least make music in the form of drum and trumpet sounds.

In Anza Borrego Desert Park, Oriflamme Mountain puts on eerie light shows. For decades people have reported seeing strange "ghost lights" in the area that appear as balls of fire that climb into the sky. Again, scientists are puzzled.

In the western Mojave Desert, the Trona Pinnacles stand as eerie spires that give the terrain the look of being on another planet. That's why the area has been used as the backdrop to many science fiction movies, from *Star Trek* to *The Planet of the Apes*.

The Ubehebe Crater in Death Valley is a major hole in the ground that extends 700 feet deep and more than a half-mile across. It's the remains of a volcano that blew its stack and imploded on itself. It's so weird that people just sit on its rim and stare.

North of Yucca Valley there is the appropriately named Giant Rock, considered the world's largest boulder. It's seven stories of stone. During the 1950s through the 1970s, it was the sight of UFO conventions. Even though a chunk of the stone broke off in 2001, the massive boulder is still considered by many to be one powerful rock.

Wild Desert:

California's deserts are a mysterious place where natural laws are often broken.

you know you're in
california when...
...lots of grapes get crushed

Go ahead. Raise a glass to toast those newlyweds, a new job, the end of a tedious workweek, or just because. The fermented beverage swilling around in your goblet most likely comes from California, a dominant force in American winemaking.

It used to be that wine country in California meant Napa Valley. That was before emerging wine regions exploded on the scene in the 1990s like popping bottles of champagne.

Now there are wine regions in every part of the state, and California wine production is as robust as a fine cabernet. California produces more than three billion bottles of wine a year, and needless to say, that's a lot of cork, too.

If California were a country, it would be the world's fourth-largest wine-producing nation. Ninety percent of all wine produced in America is coaxed to fruity perfection in California, which has more than 1,000 wineries.

California has a long history of winemaking that dates to the missions of the nineteenth century. From those humble religious roots, California's wine production is now a $45-billion industry.

Most notably, California helped repeal the snobbery once inherent in the wine-loving world. The turnaround came in the 1970s, when California wines started beating French ones for taste and quality.

Now tank-topped visitors in sandals who wouldn't know a Grenache from a Pinot Gris can stroll into a laid-back California tasting room and partake of a sampling ritual once reserved for stuck-ups cloistered in European châteaus. For a few bucks at most wineries, visitors can sniff, inspect, and taste several varieties before deciding on a purchase. Or just soak up the atmosphere and move on.

You can get even more down-and-dirty by participating in the many "stomping" festivals held around the state, where visitors are invited to help crush grapes the old-fashioned way—with their feet. It's a barrel of laughs any day.

Wineries:

If your beverage smells fruity and carries a little punch, most likely it comes from California, America's leading winemaker.

you know you're in
california when...
...you feel like you've walked into a scenic postcard

It is hard to describe the majestic beauty of Yosemite National Park. The most common reaction upon entering the park is to stand there silently, mouth agape. Words would probably ruin the moment, so it's best to shut up and stare.

Yosemite is the type of place that can turn an angry lumberjack into a peace-loving tree-hugger.

Life-changing moments are in fact common in Yosemite. Early in his life, Ansel Adams wanted to be a concert pianist. Then he got a gander at Yosemite, and before you could say "F-stop," he was on to a celebrated career as a photographer. Adams, a native San Franciscan, spent a lifetime as Yosemite's image maker, documenting in glorious black-and-white its natural grandeur.

What Adams did for Yosemite with pictures, naturalist John Muir did with words. Or tried to. Muir was so taken with Yosemite's beauty that he compared it to being in a cathedral.

Muir's persuasive writing led to the passage of an 1864 law that set aside Yosemite as the nation's first protected wilderness area. Yosemite became a national park in 1890 and now has more than 760,000 acres of protected land.

Muir and Adams were the park's two greatest champions, and their works speak con-

Yosemite National Park:

The phrase "scenic beauty" doesn't begin to describe the scenic beauty of Yosemite, which draws close to four million visitors a year.

vincingly of the park's virtues. Today the park's magnificent features speak for themselves.

There are natural attractions such as amazing hiking trails in the park's alpine wilderness, the stunning granite formations of Half Dome and El Capitan (the world's tallest unbroken cliff), and Yosemite Falls, North America's tallest waterfall at 2,425 feet.

One of the park's most unusual sites is the Ahwahnee Hotel (559–253–5635), an upscale lodging offering fluffy beds, afternoon tea service, and spa robes, smack in the middle of America's prime wilderness.

So what if purists might scoff at the idea of experiencing the great outdoors in such sumptuous digs. Let them eat beef jerky.

you know you're in
california when...
...you make nice ice

Resurfacing ice at a skating rink is not rocket science. But it's not as easy as making ice cubes, either.

You have to remove surface snow and debris, squeegee the ice and then lay down a glassy new coat that's ready for more abuse by skaters.

If you've been to a skating rink or attended a hockey game you've probably noticed the slow-moving tractorlike vehicle known as the Zamboni that emerges when an ice surface needs touching up. The Zamboni glides along in a mesmerizing circular pattern, leaving a glassy-clean ice surface in its wake.

You may have wondered if *Zamboni* means "ice maker" in Italian. It does not. *Zamboni* is actually the name of the man who created this revolutionary vehicle that brought ice resurfacing into the modern age.

The Zamboni was invented by Frank Zamboni in California in 1949. Mr. Zamboni needed a more efficient way to clean the ice at his Iceland rink in Paramount, which he had opened in 1940.

It took three workers up to ninety minutes to clean and resurface the rink after skaters had trashed the ice surface. Zamboni toyed with World War II surplus vehicles and parts to develop the prototype Zamboni Model A. It cleaned and resurfaced an ice rink in about ten minutes.

Zamboni's invention got a boost from Olympic skating champion Sonia Henie. She saw Zamboni's machine during a visit to California in 1950 and ordered two of them.

The rest is ice-resurfacing history. Today thousands of Zambonis clean and resurface ice rinks around the world. They are used by the National Hockey League and during Olympic games. The Zamboni Company is still family-owned and based in Paramount.

The Iceland rink (8041 Jackson Street; 562–633–1171; www.paramounticeland.com) is still around, too. It even displays the original Model A Zamboni. The vintage machine still works and is sometimes brought out for ceremonial work.

Zamboni:

Top speed for the Zamboni is 9 miles per hour.

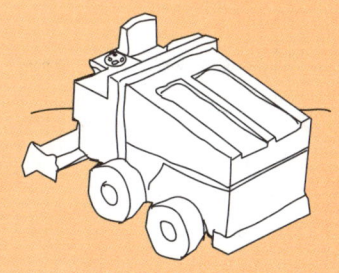

index

a
Adams, Ansel, 100
Alcatraz Island, 1
Axe, The, 2

b
Balboa bars, 3
Balboa Park, 91
barbecue, 77
Barbie dolls, 4
Beach Boys, The, 5
beach volleyball, 6
Beverly Hills, 72
Bigfoot, 7
Big Game, The, 2
Big Sur, 8
big trees, 9
bristlecone trees, 10
broadcast legends, 11
Bubble Gum Alley, 12
bullfighting, 13
Burbank, Luther, 14
Burbank Home and Gardens, 14
butterflies, 61

c
cable cars, 15
Cable Car Museum, 15
Cal and Stanford rivalry, 2
California cuisine, 16
California Academy of Tauromaquia, 13
California sea lions, 17
California State University, 43
Calistoga mud baths, 18
celebrity sightings, 19
Chez Panisse, 16
Chinatown, 20
chocolate, 21
Cobb, Robert, 22
Cobb salad, 22
cowboy culture, 23
crazy sports, 24

d
Danish culture, 82
Death Valley, 29
desert tortoise, 25
Diablo winds, 75
Disneyland, 88
Disney's California Adventure, 88
Dodgers–Giants rivalry, 26

e
earthquakes, 27
elephant seals, 28
elevation swings, 29
ethnic enclaves, 30

f
fad toys, 31
farming, 32
film industry, 33
Fort Ross, 34
freeways, 35
Frisbee, 31

g
Gap, The, 50
geeks, 79
go-karts, 85
gold, 36
gold rush, 36
Golden Gate Bridge, 37
Golden Gate Park, 91
golf, 68
grizzly bear, 38
grunion fishing, 39

h
hard-boiled detective fiction, 41
Haight-Ashbury, 40

Hearn, Chick, 11
Hearst Castle, 42
higher education, 43
hilly streets of San Francisco, The, 44
Hollywood, 33, 46
Hollywood Bowl, 45
Hollywood sign, 46
horse racing, 47
hula hoop, 31

i

Internet, The, 48
Inyo National Forest, 10

j

Jackson, Helen Hunt, 71
jazz, 49
jeans, 50
Jet Propulsion Laboratory, 51
Joshua trees, 52
Julian apple pie, 53
jumping frog jubilee, 54

k

King, Bill, 11
Knott's Berry Farm, 88

l

La Brea Tar Pits, 55
Latino culture, 56
Legoland, 88
lifeguards, 57
Lone Cypress, 58
Luther Burbank Gold Ridge Experiment Farm, The, 14
Luther Burbank Rose Parade and Festival, 14

m

massive monuments, 59
McDonald's, 60
migrations, 61
mini malls, 62
motel, the, 63

Mount Whitney, 29
Muir, John, 100
muscle beach, 64

o

oil, 65
Owens, Buck, 66

p

Palm Springs Follies, 67
Pebble Beach, 68
poppy, the, 69
presidential libraries, 70
Puck, Wolfgang, 16

r

Ramona Pageant, 71
Richard Nixon Library, 70
Rock, The, 1
Rodeo Drive, 72
Ronald Reagan Library, 70
Rose Bowl Game, 89
Russians, 34

s

San Diego Wild Animal Park, 73
San Francisco walking tours, 74
Santa Ana Winds, 75
Santa Cruz Beach Boardwalk, 76
Santa-Maria–style barbecue, 77
Scully, Vin, 11
seasons, 78
Sea World, 88
Silicon Valley, 79
Six Flags Marine World, 88
skateboarding, 80
smog, 81
Solvang, 82
sourdough bread, 83
Spanish missions, 84
speed racing, 85
Steinbeck, John, 86
Strauss, Levi, 50
Sundowners, 75

surfing, 87
swallows, 61

t
theme parks, 88
Tournament of Roses Parade, 89
Trader Joe's, 90

u
Universal Studios Hollywood, 88
University of California, 43
urban parks, 91

v
valet parking, 92
Venice, 93
Victorian architecture, 94
volcanoes, 95

w
water wars, 96
Wave, The, 97
whales, 61
wild desert, 98
wineries, 99

y
yo-yo, 31
Yosemite National Park, 100

z
Zamboni, 101
Z-boys, 80
Zephyr skate team, 80